# the connected family

# the connected family

## bridging the digital generation gap

## seymour papert

foreword by nicholas negroponte

LONGSTREET PRESS
Atlanta, Georgia

Published by
LONGSTREET PRESS, INC.
A subsidiary of Cox Newspapers,
A subsidiary of Cox Enterprises, Inc.
2140 Newmarket Parkway
Suite 118
Marietta, GA 30067

Printed in the United States of America

1st printing 1996

Library of Congress Catalog Card Number: 96-76500

ISBN: 1-56352-335-3

Film preparation by Overflow Graphics Inc., Forest Park, Georgia

Jacket and book design by Fabrizio La Rocca
Typesetting by Jill Dible

*To Ian, John, Mason, Sam and*
*their grandmother, Suzanne Massie*

# Contents

# Foreword

Never before have we had so much to learn from kids, and we admit it. We all turned to children to program our VCRs, but that was a means to outsmart those nasty and heartless manufacturers who even made the buttons kid-sized. Twice a year, all homes in America have their digital time put forward or back, mostly by children, not because it is too hard for an adult, but because it is just not worth the effort to learn and remember how to change the oven clock. Plus we don't find it much fun.

Something very different is happening with computers and the Internet. Children are no longer just an adult's prosthetic tool to cope with electro-mechanical gadgetry. Instead, kids bring a new culture to the family landscape, a culture which has at its core the extremes of being simultaneously personal and global. Children understand computers because they can control them. They love them because they can make their own windows of interest. Remember sitting in class? If what the teacher said was too simple, you lost interest. If it was too hard, you lost interest. And oh how tiny that window was.

Seymour shows the reader a different window, one which opens as wide as you want. He argues that it cannot be left shut. In some sense, Seymour allows you to be an atheist, but not an agnostic. He is soft spoken and patient in real life, and between the lines as well. While he would never say it this way, he is telling children to beware of parents who try to colonialize the computer medium. He is telling parents to beware of some of their deepest feelings, even to pinch themselves now and again, when they fall back on drill and practice in the three R's. But wait, the three R's worked for me. Right?

Wrong. In today's world, most adults would do very badly as kids. There are many more complexities, ambiguities and differences. This is not because we have traffic jams, gutless politicians or racial tension, but because we have an information access which reaches across the planet. And now it is not only available to banks, airlines and media moguls, but to children as well. Kids can empower themselves and see new notions of work and play, society and self, teaching and learning—concepts which no longer have those crisp lines separating one from the other.

I have known Seymour for over thirty years. More than anything, he taught me how to think. In 1965 he wrote the foreword to Warren McCulloch's *Embodiments of Mind*, which was the only part of the book I really understood. About that time we became friends. We cooked together, we traveled together and we even got ourselves in trouble once in a while. I wondered if I would ever be able to write a foreword for somebody as great. Now I got my chance. This is a man who makes remarks like, "You can't think about thinking unless you think about thinking about something." That keeps you thinking.

When I first read this book I heard Seymour's voice and recognized his expressions. Then I realized that my reaction was not so personal: Others will hear the same voice of intelligence, experience and passion. They will understand immediately that these are not the thoughts of somebody who just bought a PC ten years ago, but of somebody deeply involved in the issues raised here, from his childhood days in South Africa to his studies in England, from his work with mentor Jean Piaget to his partner Marvin Minsky to his recent decade at the M.I.T. Media Lab, where I have had the honor to work with him.

Seymour is the emancipated child.

*Nicholas Negroponte, August 1996*

# the connected family

# Generations

## A Love Affair

Across the world there is a passionate love affair between children and computers. I have worked with children and computers in Africa and Asia and America, in cities, in suburbs, on farms and in jungles. I have worked with poor children and rich children; with children of bookish parents and with children from illiterate families. But these differences don't seem to matter. Everywhere, with very few exceptions, I see the same gleam in their eyes, the same desire to appropriate this thing. And more than wanting it, they seem to know that in a deep way it already belongs to them. They know they can master it more easily and more naturally than their parents. They know they are the computer generation.

Like other passionate affairs of the young, this one mystifies thoughtful parents and troubles cautious ones—often even parents who are computer enthusiasts themselves. And so it should. The computer presence will undoubtedly transform the lives of children, and if we are entitled to *hope* the change will be beneficial we are not entitled to *assume* this on behalf of the next generation. Great change is never free and seldom comes without risk.

Benefits and dangers seem to come in pairs. Parents are delighted when their children spend hours with a computer in deep concentration. But they feel nervous about an addictive quality of the experience. They wonder whether video games do harm beyond merely wasting time.

Parents are amazed and excited to see children break down the barrier of space and nationality, making pen friends across the globe or becoming experts on the planet's environment. But then they worry about whether children might fall into bad company or pick up corrupting ideas while roaming the highways and byways of cyberspace.

Most parents are pleased when their children acquire knowledge they never had themselves, but many feel alienated and rejected when their children talk in language they do not understand about exotic places and engrossing activities they do not know. Some wonder whether living in an artificial world will sap childhood's innocent spontaneity.

Some parents are worried, and many more ought to be, about the fact that profit-driven barons of the software industry can have as much influence as they do on the minds and the **culture of children**.

To begin thinking more deeply about why so many children are passionate about computers and why so many parents are nervous, I take a look at the beginnings of learning and how they might be changing.

# Freedom Lost

Watch a baby explore the world. Everything within sight is seen, everything within touch is felt by hand, by foot and by mouth. The full range of available sounds is emitted. The baby is exploring a small world, but is exploring it very thoroughly. It is obvious that a great deal is being learned. Educators talking about the way the learning happens would use words like: self-directed, experiential, nonverbal. I prefer to say **home-style learning**.

Gradually the child becomes aware of a much larger world that cannot be reached and explored in this way. Known people are sometimes in other places. Sights are fleetingly seen from a car window. Books have pictures of animals from other continents. Increasingly, questions come up that cannot be answered by direct exploration. There are not many ways open to find answers. Essentially three: Think up an answer, ask someone or just wait in the hope that one day someone in person or on television will give the answer.

And so little by little the child's ways of getting knowledge and of using it are forced to change, to become more dependent on other people and less spontaneous; more verbal and less experiential. The shift is not emotionally neutral. In fact it runs into head-on collision with the development of a sense of delight in "doing it myself." More in some cases than in others but always to some extent, the change brings elements of frustration and anger.

That is how it was. A story hints at how it will be.

A LEARNING STORY

# Ian Views a Videotape

My grandson Ian, aged about three at the time, walked over to a shelf where videotapes were kept. He selected one (although he "couldn't read" he could choose the tape he wanted), loaded it into the VCR, sat down in a comfortable armchair, wielded the remote control, uttered a child's expletive I understood a moment later as meaning he had forgotten to rewind the tape the last time he used it, rewound, pressed PLAY and settled in to watch the tape. It was about road-making machinery—a topic of great interest to many children, and not only boys.

My first reaction was to be astonished by the **fluency** with which Ian did all this. Then on reflection I decided there really wasn't anything astonishing in it except my own astonishment—on which it is worth pausing for a moment because it shows that even someone who has spent half a lifetime studying children can fall into underestimating their capacities, and that observing children using technology reminds us that they can do more than we think. In fact I have come to see parents' expanding ideas about what children can do as one of the important contributions of computers to how children learn. The more they are respected the better they will do.

What Ian actually did with the mechanics of the technology was no more complex than some of the operations performed by every three-year-old without arousing one bit of astonishment. Knowing where a favorite toy is kept, getting it out and putting it away later is quite as complex a performance as using a VCR or loading a CD-ROM into the computer drive and clicking icons until the desired action is produced. Getting around the house is much more complex than managing the icons on a computer screen, and getting around the parents infinitely so.

Yet there *was* a good reason to be astonished.

What impresses me most in the incident is not related to the mechanics of handling the VCR but to the content of the experience. My mind was boggled by how different Ian's simple act of choosing and viewing a videotape was from anything people my age could do when we were three years old. The nearest I could have come to immersing myself for half an hour in a topic like road-making machines would have been to find an adult with the knowledge, the storytelling talent and the time and inclination to tell me about it. For this I was dependent on adults. As it happens I was especially lucky in having a scientifically educated father willing to spend a lot of time talking with me. But my freedom of choice was far short of what a collection of tapes, CD-ROMs and Web addresses can give a child today, and this in turn is far, far short of what children will have in a few years' time.

With greater freedom of choice will come dramatic change in how children learn and develop.

# . . . and Freedom Regained

Ian may have been born a little too soon for the changes to be really dramatic. Although he often used them, his collection of tapes was far too small to have anything of relevance to most of what might attract his interest. For example, during the week after his fish died, he grabbed every adult he could to ask questions and talk about it. But imagine a situation in which he could have found easy and flexible access to information and artificial realities relevant to fish and dying. It seems obvious that he would have spent significant time exploring his curiosity and his feelings by immersion in these.

Of course I am not implying that it would be better for a child to go to a machine than to a person when troubled by the death of his fish—quite the contrary. I am seriously worried about the psychological and spiritual consequences of children becoming more independent of their parents in their exploration of the world. But for better or for worse this will happen, and it will be far more likely to happen for the worse if parents act like **cyberostriches**, putting their heads in the sand in denial of the looming changes in the learning environment.

Children driven by instincts for independent action and frustrated by dependency in learning are seizing with passion the key to freedom in learning. Parents can fight it or join it. *The Connected Family* is really about strategies for the sensible choice. About how you can "join it."

Over many generations, societies have evolved ways of relating to children. These have become embedded in cultures as the principles of good parenting. But now assumptions on which they were based are unraveling as unprecedented opportunities are opening to children. It may seem to be an awesome task to rethink and rebuild our ideas about children and how to deal with them. It will certainly require some work. But it is the task we have to face, and facing it one step at a time is not really awesome at all. I shall offer you an approach to it that may sometimes be a little hard but will also be enjoyable. Using language I have learned from children engaged with computers, it is **hard fun**.

## Hypertext

You have noticed that some words are underlined. This is not for emphasis but in the spirit of what is called hypertext in computer jargon. If you were reading this on a computer screen the underlining (or some similar indication) would tell you that the word **hypertext** is a hot word, which means that something interesting will happen if you click on it with your mouse. Perhaps a definition of the word or a bunch of other hot spots that lead you to related passages might jump onto the screen, or perhaps a voice would give you the same information or perhaps an animated cartoon would play out the meaning of the word.

Although text printed on paper is not active in this way, I shall mark some words as **hot** to advise you that there is more about that idea somewhere in the book. You can consult the Hot Word Index to find the other places, or simply take the underlining as meaning "Don't worry if this concept is unfamiliar . . . as you read on, more meaning for it will build up."

■

# Intentions

I first thought about writing a book like this one while talking to the zillionth mother who asked me whether she should buy a computer for her children and what kind and what the children should do with it at what ages and which was the best software. It was easy to recognize a heartfelt need for guidance and reassurance, but I still had to grapple with tougher problems about the form the book should take.

Asking parents what they thought they needed suggested two models: Benjamin Spock and *Consumer Reports*. A book that might be called *Dr. Spock for the Computer Generation* would answer questions about such issues as appropriate ages and amounts of time in front of the screen, and the dangers of gender bias and addiction and pornography. A *Consumer Report* would attempt to rate the tens of thousands (I mean this quite literally!) of products that vie for the minds of children and the dollars of their parents. Many of the parents who suggested these models for my book were expressing dissatisfaction with the advice and reviews they read in magazines or on-line or indeed in books. One put it to me like this:

> When the reviewers like a software, they are full of gush such as: "easy to use," "marvelous graphics," "children love it," "lots of learning." When you talk you raise more controversial questions. Half the time I can't agree with you but you get me thinking. Something important is affecting our children. What we need is not being told it's good, it's bad or it gets four stars like a restaurant. We need to talk more, argue more, think more about what lies behind it all.

They made doing a book like this sound attractive, but I was not convinced and kept looking for another format.

Turning my inquiry from the parents to their children suggested a very (perhaps shockingly) different model. An email from a group of high school students is exceptional only in its eloquence:

> Those of us who own a PC know one problem very well: Most parents are pretty slow in understanding the PC. To them even the easiest steps of using a word processor have to be explained for hours again and again. And although these parents really want to learn they fail; computer courses also often cannot help. This usually

7

leads to resignation on both sides: We, the young ones, regard the old as inferior, and the older generations regard the young as arrogant and unable to really explain and teach. . . .

. . . adults must first really open up to new matters, they must not tell themselves they could not learn anymore, and they have to recreate self-directed exploration. Otherwise they will not be able to catch up with their children's speed of learning.

It is not remarkable that adolescents are critical of their parents. What is really remarkable is that the views they express here are not confined to adolescents. I increasingly hear very similar views from much younger children and, most significantly, from the parents themselves. Many adults would agree that in their own dealings with computers they show symptoms of what a school psychologist would call a learning disability. It is becoming a cultural cliché that adults are inferior to children in learning about computers and, as often happens, the judgment of inferiority becomes a self-fulfilling prophecy.

I was influenced by all three suggestions for what the book should contain, but it is the youngsters who put their finger on what is most important. *What parents most need to know about computers is not really about computers but about learning.*

That sounds commonplace: Everyone knows computers help children learn. But I was coming to understand that most parents will do better at sharing and enhancing their children's learning if *they take a hard look at their own learning*: Many need to work at their learning habits; most—even those who are adept at using computers—should learn new computer skills; and almost all should work at uncovering assumptions that make them want to impose on their children the content and learning methods of their own school days.

These thoughts led me to look around for other recent examples of large-scale change in people's attitudes to their own learning. One of my favorite examples is cooking.

Back in the 1950s, it was a rare American who did not hold "French" or "gourmet" cooking in the kind of awe that computers would arouse thirty years later. Television became the key medium for the turnaround in attitude, not because it was a good medium for disseminating recipes (books are better) but because it made attitudes and feelings visible. I bet that a large proportion of my readers know the incident when Julia Child accidentally dropped her duck in front of the live cameras, calmly picked it up, dusted it off and went on with her cooking demonstration. By entering the cultural consciousness of middle-class America, such incidents contributed significantly to demystifying and "de-snobbing" the mystique of *haute cuisine*, and to bringing tens of millions of Americans to expand what they were prepared to learn and do in the kitchen.

Looking at one not-untypical family will hint at what a similar turnaround in attitudes towards computers might be like.

> For Lisa, the computer has become a "home wrecker," separating her from husband Ron as well as from the children. When she is ready for bed, Ron is reading email, exploring the Internet or struggling with some new "installation" (a word she has never been able to grasp) on his computer. Her feelings have evolved from indulgent interest to resentment to full-fledged anger. And her sense of isolation is aggravated by sensing a growing gap between herself and her children, who so easily master software that leaves her with a feeling of baffled inferiority.

On the face of it there is a world of difference between the technophobic Lisa, who simply won't touch a computer, and the technophilic Ron, whose late-night adventures on the Internet are threatening their marriage. As Lisa sees it, Ron loves the computer, loves pounding those keys and loves buying it the latest software and fanciest gadgets. In response, her long-standing reticence towards technology has developed into feelings usually reserved for a human rival.

Yet a closer look will show that the difference between Lisa and Ron might not be as great as it seems: Lisa in fact has much more know-how relevant to technology than she thinks she does, and in some situations people like Ron show irrational phobias about technology that are not very different from Lisa's. My approach to Lisa is exactly the opposite of a television advertisement for an Internet service, in which a woman says, "I don't need to understand technology. I just need to know that it works for my family." The advertisement is meant to reassure and perhaps does so in the short term, but in the long run it mystifies. I'd rather have the woman say, "Like most adult Americans, I know enough about technology to start exploring cyberspace with my family and once we are there, little by little, my children and I will enjoy learning more. . . ."

The truth is that with the right learning attitude, Lisa would need little effort to understand this technology and even enjoy doing so. And besides, she would also enjoy her children more (and perhaps serve as a better role model) by sharing a richer experience with them.

My first strategy for helping Lisa change her attitude is very close to Julia Child's dropping of the duck—and the opposite of what the TV commercial tried to tell her. The fact is that the technology won't always "work," and telling people like Lisa that it is really very simple and foolproof leads them to think they must be technological fools when it doesn't work. Much better to help her understand that this marvelous technology is being brought out into the world in a very primitive state. When something goes wrong don't blame yourself; blame **Bill Gates** and keep going. There's usually a way around the problem.

Finding a way around the problem might require time. I am very fond of quoting M. Scott Peck's description in *The Road Less Traveled* of how he was cured of believing he "was deficient in some gene, or by curse of nature lacking some mystical quality responsible for mechanical ability." One day, he writes, "I happened upon a neighbor in the process of repairing a lawn mower. After greeting him I remarked, 'Boy, I sure admire you. I've never been able to fix those kinds of things or do anything like that.' My neighbor, without a moment's hesitation, shot back, 'That's because you don't take the time.'" Soon after that Peck was faced with a jammed hand brake. Looking under the dashboard, he saw "a confusing jumble of wires and tubes and rods." In the past his response would have been to pull and push here and there and quickly give up. This time, remembering the neighbor's words, he gave the problem the time it needed. Gradually the jumble began to make sense. Eventually he saw that an ounce of pressure in the right place would release the brake, and he emerged with the wonderful feeling that "I was a master mechanic!"

A big part of what I'd like Lisa to learn is a sense of how long finding her way around the technology takes. I don't want to urge her to devote all her time whenever something goes wrong. I myself sometimes call in a repair person, who finds out after two hours that all I needed to do was something that takes five minutes. But she would have a better relationship with her children if she sometimes solved a computer problem herself . . . or with them.

I'd also like to encourage Lisa to push her use of the computer just a little beyond loading and running an "easy-to-use" piece of software. Lisa uses America Online somewhat diffidently to send email and watches her five-year-old use a "paint program" such as KidPix to draw on the screen. But she does not think of putting these activities together by helping the child send a birthday picture across the Internet to a family member. Perhaps by the time you read this you will have a turnkey software that does just that—in which case you would have to invent a different exercise to make my point. As far as I know, at this time Lisa would have to stretch herself a little, to the extent of using the paint program to save the picture, then switching to AOL and knowing how to attach a file to an email. She would not have to stretch very much, since the five-year-old will be able to do this herself very soon. I just think it would be good for the child to learn this kind of operation from (or better, with) her mother, and good for the mother to get into the habit of going beyond what is written in the instruction manual.

Let's turn now to Ron. It might seem that his need for advice on children and computers is diametrically different from Lisa's. His fluent mastery of Windows, spreadsheets and word processors leads you to think that he would be utterly fearless in facing the most formidable software. But just whisper something like "programming," and surprisingly many people like Ron immediately go into a blue funk, though the ideas behind this scary word are far more intelligible and learnable than the baroque intricacies of the software that Ron uses every day.

One group of people that programming never terrifies is children. Children take to programming like ducks to water, especially if they are offered a gentle approach to it. In *The Connected Family* I use programming as one of several activities that needn't be branded as knowledge reserved for nerdy specialists. Once any activity is so branded, its inaccessibility to ordinary folk becomes a self-fulfilling prophecy. The message goes out that it is terrifying, so people tremble instead of trying. Books about it use language that is appropriate only to specialists. Indeed the activity itself evolves into forms that serve the purposes of specialists rather than those of a wider public. Far from being terrified and influenced by these preconceptions, children want to learn to program because they seek mastery. Since it is paradoxical and even perverse to allow adult fears to stand in their way, I have a proposition for both Ron and Lisa. It's an invitation to join me in

Chapter 6 for a programming party. Try it once before you decide it's not for you.

I want to reassure parents about psychological as well as technical matters. Many look with awe at the choice of what to do with the new technology to help their children. With no training in child development or psychology, they feel they have no basis for their personal judgment, especially when it goes against the opinions of experts (including me). If you are one of these, my message is that while your attitude shows an admirable sense of responsibility it is really mistaken. Your intuitive sense of people and your own experience are rich mines of psychological knowledge. A lot of what I have to say is really aimed at helping you feel confident enough to use what you know.

Paradoxically, to achieve this reassuring goal I sometimes have to be a gadfly, using a sting to jolt people out of a gullibility that flies in the face of what common sense and experience tell them. Not surprisingly, this gullibility is exploited, and at the same time reinforced, by a software industry that has taken shape under influences other than the best thinking about learning. It was almost inevitable that the design and marketing of products would play to the lowest denominator of parental concepts of good learning. To counteract this I cannot evaluate individual products one by one. Instead I offer a perspective within which each of you can generate answers that match your own values and your own sense of where you and your family are going. The answers will not and should not be the same for everyone. I recall what might be the wisest among Benjamin Spock's thousands of recommendations: "Remember, I know nothing about your children. You know everything."

Developing your own personal perspective will not come without effort, though I cannot say how much. What I *can* advise is what I read in every article about fitness and exercise: Feel out a sustainable level that you can keep up over the long haul.

The later chapters of *The Connected Family* are a guide to two kinds of relevant activities. One kind is about computer projects including, among others, the programming party. Doing these activities, you and your kids can teach one another and learn from one another. As a mature adult you will be able to bring something to the learning table whatever the ages of your children. But they will eventually learn faster than you and know more than you about some aspects of whatever you are doing together. *What is important is to use the kids as a resource and to remember that they will be there to help you if you just learn to let them—which does not mean you won't also be helping them.*

Working together on these projects will help family members understand and respect one another's **learning styles** and different kinds of computer expertise. With time will come greater confidence by adults in what the younger ones can do to contribute to the life of the family. **Nicholas Negroponte** remarks in his foreword to *The Connected Family* that many families rely on the kids to handle the VCR. Familiarity with the Internet can open vast new opportunities for children to take on responsibilities.

Some examples: I need to buy a car and have spent several hours searching on the Web for information about recommended models. It took almost no time to get information from manufacturers' Web pages, but more time and patience was needed to find chat groups and news groups which yielded relevant facts and perspectives as well as the names of some other models worth considering. I am sure that an eight-year-old could have saved me the time and done a better job. I have a friend whose children have researched vacation trips down to the details of getting pictures of hotels and their prices as well as airline schedules for various options. I have another friend who finds on the breakfast table a printout of news items that broke too late for the morning paper. Many families now send Christmas and birthday cards made by children. I could continue indefinitely spinning out examples, but

I stop here because I would never do as well as what would emerge in time in your own family.

Although all these jobs could in principle have been done without computers, the technology means that they are more likely to be done and, if they are, to be carried out effectively and to professional standards.

The other kind of activity is more political than technological. The **learning culture** of your home will sooner or later have to make connections with learning cultures outside. We'll touch on many of these: the many cultures of the Internet, the families of your children's friends and, most seriously, the culture of school.

Although your immediate purpose in trying to influence schools will probably be the welfare of your own children, doing so will also make you part of an important social movement. In my earlier books on computers and learning I focused on schools, and seldom found it necessary to discuss computers in the home—school was where the action was, and the small number of students with home computers was a negligible factor in school change.

The situation is rapidly turning around as computer usage in schools lags quite dramatically behind the development of home computing. This is obviously true in a *quantitative* sense: There are now many more computers in homes than in schools, and an increasing number of students spend more time on computer-supported learning activities at home than at school. It is also true in a *qualitative* sense: The best uses of computers that I have seen in homes are so much better than what is being done with computers in most schools that I have come to see home computing as a major (perhaps *the* major) source of pressure for educational reform. I cannot hide the fact that one of my intentions here is wanting to support this pressure.

Finally I mention one last intention: a message to those parents whose children are given labels suggesting that they need "special education" to deal with learning disabilities. Although I devote only a few pages specifically to this issue, it is really the main topic of every page I write. I am convinced that a large proportion (though certainly not all) of cases of learning difficulty are produced by imposing on children ways of learning that go against their personal **styles**. Over and over again I have seen children shake off their apparent disabilities when given the opportunity to learn in a way that comes naturally to them. What I see as the real contribution of digital media to education is a flexibility that could allow every individual to find personal paths to learning. This will make it possible for the dream of every progressive educator to come true: In the learning environment of the future, every learner will be "special."

# Technology

## Cybertopians and Cybercritics

Parents are not the only ones who are nervous about the coming digital world. We are all being assailed by proclamations and predictions of a computer future in which everything imaginable is changed by the digital revolution. We all wish we had a crystal ball to tell us what this future will be.

Droves of futurists are eager to tell us, but they speak with conflicting voices. Cybertopians praise the wonders of the digital age. Cybercritics warn of dire dangers. The sides agree only that we haven't seen anything yet: For good or for bad what we see today is a pale imitation of what is to come.

Where do I stand?

I cannot align myself with either the utopians or the critics. Both are right. Both are wrong.

In a superficial sense both sides are right. The utopians are absolutely right in their belief that the digital revolution offers opportunities for a better life. In fact its implications for children could go far beyond what any of the recent spate of utopian books promise. But opportunities are not always turned to advantage. When critics look at what people are actually doing, they are easily able to show that many have put out money, time and high hopes for very little return. Indeed many are worse off than without the technology. We have to find a better approach than taking sides.

I am not going to broach the Big Question of how computers will change society as a whole. I shall focus on what some may see as just one issue—learning—but it is one that increasingly many are coming to see as the most important single issue facing society as we move into the next millennium.

To skeptics who might ridicule seeing learning as the most important issue in a deeply troubled world, I will only say that none of the world's troubles will be resolved unless people, especially those of the next generation, learn to think in better ways than those who brought the troubles about. Having said this I shall from now on confine myself to far more specific and immediate questions about what changes in how people learn may come about via the computer. These are not simply changes in curriculums or test scores. They include changes in the human relationships most closely related to learning—relationships between generations in families, relationships between teachers and learners and relationships between peers with common interests. The debates between utopians and critics are as fierce in this "limited" arena as anywhere.

I am convinced that the way children learn will improve dramatically and often find myself fighting fiercely with those who say computers have little to offer in this area or will do actual harm by immersing children in artificial worlds at the expense of spending time with nature. Yet when I visit a school, ninety-nine times out of a hundred I cringe. What is actually being done there is a sheer travesty of what could be done with the technology. So I often find myself fighting just as fiercely with people who thought they agreed with me about the importance of technology in education and are surprised to find me being obstreperous about how it is done.

For example, learning multiplication by putting flash cards on the screen is not a new way of learning math. It is a polished-up version of the old ways and promotes to greater heights their worst and most mechanical features. Moreover it is often done in a spirit that I see as dangerously dishonest: Disguising flash cards as a **game** introduces an element of **deception** that undermines two fundamental educational principles.

First, learning works best when the learner is a willing and conscious participant. Second, deception and dishonesty in the teaching process make a mockery of the idea that schools should develop moral values as well as knowledge of math or history. One of my themes in *The Connected Family* is that truth in learning is no less important—indeed far more so—than truth in advertising or any other grown-up endeavor. And one of the big contributions of the computer is the opportunity for children to experience the thrill of chasing after knowledge they really want.

I am no Pollyanna about technology. The record of how society took up earlier technologies is frighteningly bad. We first made automobiles in the hundreds of millions and then worried about how to mend the damage done by deforming our cities, polluting our atmosphere and changing the lives of our teenage children. Why should we as a society do better this time?

I don't know whether digital technology can hurt the atmosphere. But I do know that it could make a dramatic difference for the better or for the worse in the lives of children, and that there is no guarantee that it will be for the good. Quite the contrary, if one goes by what one sees happening today, it is almost guaranteed that the technology will be used mindlessly or for the profit of corporations rather than for the benefit of children.

tions—they developed an interest in the subject and increased their test scores. Teresa M. introduced a new twist by organizing the students into companies and letting them choose subjects they found interesting.

One group chose the anatomy of a slug. I am sure their reasons included the kind of interest in yucky things we saw in Lisa and Mark. But they also had an educational idea, which was emphasized in the explanation they wrote for teachers about why this topic should be studied: "At school they make us study the anatomy of animals like frogs. But this is too easy because you can see all the parts and they look like ours. The slug is more interesting because you have to think more." What impressed me was that the students were thinking about learning.

---

# "Now I know why we have nouns and verbs."

A group of "average" seventh-grade students were at work on what they called "computer poetry" by making computer programs generate sentences like:

INSANE RETARD MAKES BECAUSE SWEET SNOOPY SCREAMS
SEXY WOLF LOVES THAT WHY THE SEXY LADY HATES
UGLY MAN LOVES BECAUSE UGLY DOG HATES
MAD WOLF HATES BECAUSE INSANE WOLF SKIPS
SEXY RETARD SCREAMS THAT'S WHY THE SEXY RETARD HATES
THIN SNOOPY RUNS BECAUSE FAT WOLF HOPS
SWEET FOGINY SKIPS A FAT LADY RUNS

JENNY'S "CONCRETE POETRY"

One of the students, a thirteen-year-old named Jenny, had deeply touched the project's staff by asking on the first day of her computer work, "Why were we chosen for this? We're not the brains." One day she came in very excited about a discovery. "Now I know why we have nouns and verbs," she said.

For many years in school Jenny had been drilled in grammatical categories. She had never understood the differences between nouns and verbs and adverbs. But now it was apparent that her difficulty with grammar was not due to an inability to work with logical categories. It was something else. She had simply seen no purpose in the enterprise. She had not been able to make any sense of what grammar was about in the sense of what it might be for. And when she had asked what it was for, the explanations that her teachers gave seemed manifestly dishonest. She said she had been told that "grammar helps you talk better."

But Jenny didn't see any way in which grammar could help talking, nor did she think her talking needed any help. Therefore she learned to approach grammar with resentment. And, as is the case for most of us, resentment guaranteed failure. But now, as she tried to get the computer to generate poetry, something remarkable happened. She found herself classifying words into categories, not because she had been told she had to but because she needed to. In order to "teach" her computer to make strings of words that would look like English, she had to "teach" it to choose words of an appropriate class.

What she learned about grammar from this experience with a machine was anything but mechanical. She not only "understood" grammar, she changed her relationship to it. It was "hers," and during her year with the computer, incidents like this helped Jenny change her image of herself. Her performance changed too; her previously low to average grades became "straight As" for her remaining years of school. She learned that she could be a "brain" after all.

# Cyberostrich

The story of how Jenny learned grammar pinpoints a common weakness of educational software intended for schools as well as for home use. Most of what is on the market sets out to teach the facts and skills of a subject like grammar (or math or geography) much as human teachers and textbooks have traditionally done. But Jenny got something very different out of her experience. The computer did not directly *teach* her any grammar. Its contribution was to dissolve barriers to learning grammar by allowing her to find meaning for it as a **powerful idea** —one that she could use, and in a project she had invented herself. Thereafter learning grammar would be something she would approach with enthusiasm, however it was taught. What the computer experience gave her was far more valuable than any improvement in teaching a fixed curriculum.

I have heard the objection that the computer does not deserve credit for making grammar useful because Jenny used grammar every time she spoke. But this confuses two kinds of grammatical knowledge. The source of Jenny's problem was that the formal grammar taught in school fell so far short of her intuitive grammatical knowledge that she really could not put the formal grammar to any use. The computer gets credit for providing a medium in which she could use her formal knowledge while it was catching up with its intuitive counterpart. Thus the computer bypasses school's traditional mixture of artificial motivation and imposed discipline to "get" children to learn material that they can't use.

I give the title **ostrich** to educators who are excited by the prospect that computers will improve what they do in schools but hide their heads in the sand to avoid seeing that these technologies will inexorably give rise to megachange that goes far beyond improvement.

I use a parable to give a sharper sense of how the **techno-ostrich** thinks:

In 1800 a techno-ostrich conceived the idea of a jet engine and imagined using it to augment the power of horses, so stagecoaches could cross the continent in half the time.

The jet engine was a brilliant idea which actually was invented before the development of aviation created a need for it. I don't suppose that anyone actually proposed using it to augment horses, but any uses that anyone might have imagined would have been about as impractical in those days and, since real people are not that silly, in fact it was not used at all. The silliness of the techno-ostrich in the story is that he (it had to be a man!) was determined to use the new idea but could think of using it only in the framework of the transportation system as he knew it: wagons, sail ships and the like. He lacked the creative imagination to see that the jet engine could only come into its own in the context of a radically changed idea about transportation.

This is exactly where we stand in the use of computers by schools. The **cyberostriches** who make school policy are determined to use computers but can only imagine using them in the framework of the school system as they know it: children following a predetermined curriculum mapped out year by year and lesson by lesson. This is quite perverse: new technology being used to strengthen a poor method of education that was invented only because there were no computers when school was designed.

# Cameras and Cultures

There is nothing bizarre or wrong with the first use of a new technology being an aid to old ways of doing things. What is wrong with educational uses of the computer is not that they started that way, but that many are stalled there at a time when we already know how to move on to better things. Let's compare this situation with an older one—the movies—where a technological innovation gave rise to something very new.

The first idea of making a movie was to put the camera in front of a stage and film a play that was acted as if for a live audience.

The difference between theater + camera and what developed from it is an excellent analogy for thinking about what I hope will happen in education. One line of development was technological: Cameras became better, movies turned into talkies, Technicolor brightened the screen and eventually the electronic revolution opened the vast world of video. But as impressive as the technological development might be, another kind of development was ultimately more interesting and important.

What grew out of the first movies is best described as a new **culture**. The stuff of which it was made included very new artistic techniques (for example the *close-up* was an entirely new concept and initially resisted by actors), the social role of "stars" and indeed the phenomenon of Hollywood, with its extravagances, its hype, its Academy Awards, its idiosyncratic personalities and its enormous influence on people all over the world.

We can take the cinema story as a model for understanding the story of computers in education. The story reminds us that we should expect slow growth of new ideas (for cultures never grow fast). It also warns us to be on guard against being stuck in the "theater + camera" stage. It leads us to expect resistance by educators to new techniques but it also suggests that we ourselves should resist the spread of Hollywood hype into the marketing of educational computer products.

# Literacy and Fluency

Computer literacy has become a catch phrase of the decade, and current wisdom says that if children grow up without it they will be unemployable in the job market of the future.

There is *some* truth in this, but how much depends on how you define computer literacy. In fact as it is understood in most discussions of school policy, it carries far more **deception** than truth. The content of the typical computer literacy curriculum is a grab bag of superficial knowledge about the parts of a computer and current office software selected primarily because it is easy to teach with very limited numbers of computers. The word "literacy" is misapplied. The knowledge acquired is so shallow that someone who knew the equivalent amount about reading and writing and books would be called *illiterate* rather than literate. It would be as if someone knew the names of the letters but could not read, or could answer such questions as what is a book and what is a library but had never read a book or used a library. The kids coming out of computer literacy courses are profoundly illiterate in relation to what really matters about computers: that you can use them for your own purposes.

In fairness to school officials I quickly note that believing such courses could be helpful for future employment comes from superficial thinking rather than from dishonesty. Most officials simply do not know enough about computers and their uses to recognize their policies as a cruel deception of children whose only access to computers is through the school. However, exonerating the officials does not put right policies that are fundamentally wrong. I don't just mean that the computer literacy curriculum is not quite good enough; I mean that it is exactly in the wrong direction.

Thinking about this strong statement will be a good warm-up for Chapter 6, where I invite you to try out computer skills you might want to adopt (and adapt) for yourself and your family. There are several differences between the spirit of these chapters and what I see in most school computer literacy programs. Most important, I did not try to choose skills that might be valuable for getting jobs in some hypothetical future. I chose skills that will be valuable right now for getting the most out of living and learning in the present.

Obviously this policy of selection does not mean neglecting the future. Quite the contrary, it is aimed at helping children learn about many more important and long-lasting topics than office computer skills that will certainly be obsolete long before these kids get anywhere near the job-seeking age. Among these are some topics that have always been included in school's traditional curriculum (for example, communication and mathematics), topics that ought to be included (for example, the study of learning as a skill) and my own collection of computer skills very different from what you find in a typical computer literacy curriculum (for example, something I call **technological fluency**).

The word **fluent** expresses the most important aspect of the kind of knowledge children should have about technology. There is a big difference between having a lot of school knowledge about a language and being fluent in it. I know people who never had less than an "A" in French and can tell you about forms of verbs but would have trouble asking in a Parisian supermarket where the detergents are. Most courses in computer literacy end up with students who know a lot of facts about computers and ways of using them. But when they find themselves in an unfamiliar situation, they grope and stumble like an unfluent person looking for the right word in a foreign language.

The way you get to be fluent in using technology is like the way you get to be fluent in French. Fluency comes from use. Being fluent in a language never comes from school-book exercises. It comes from struggling to express yourself in the language in a lot of different situations. And, by the way, it does not mean that you never make mistakes. People that are very fluent in a language might still make mistakes such as using "that" instead of "who" in a sentence like this one. And being fluent with computers doesn't mean that you know everything. In fact good evidence of your technological fluency would be what you do when you don't know how something works. The technologically unfluent person becomes embarrassed or runs for help. The technologically fluent

28

person will hit a few keys until something happens, probably not what was wanted, and go smoothly from there to home in on getting the right thing to happen.

Children often amaze their parents by their technological fluency. While father is being driven crazy trying to get his newest software to work, Lauren, age eight, looking over his shoulder, says "let me try," and in no time a menu has been pulled down, the mouse clicked on one of the entries and the software is up and running.

How did she do this? Is it true that children have a magical connection with the right way to do things with computers? No, there is nothing magical about it except for the magical way that children learn. Lauren's biggest asset is not being afraid to try something. But this does not mean trying just any old thing. Lauren knows from experience that certain keys are more likely to bring interesting results. The father's fear of doing something wrong inhibits exploration that would lead to finding the right action.

Another way to look at this is as a failure to appreciate the value of imprecise knowledge. When the kid tries something that doesn't get the desired result on first shot, the parent will sometimes think, "well, he isn't that smart after all." But the kid will still beat him to the answer. If this seems illogical, think of the following example that isn't about computers and is so simple that you might think it ridiculous, but it makes the point.

> In the building in which I work, the elevators have a security code after office hours. My way of remembering the codes is to get it approximately. Say the new decode is 2951. Typically what I remember is something like "it's got 51 and 29 in it." So I might try 5129 and fail before trying 2951 and succeeding. Why should I burden myself with more information than I really need? Only school tests define knowing as getting it exactly right on the first

29

shot. Most places in life, knowing enough to know you can get there is all you need.

Kids like Lauren acquire fluency by playing with a lot of different software packages ranging from games to surfing the Internet. They use the Internet to download dozens or hundreds of free software titles. They often have no interest in the software itself except to find out what it's about and how to use it. In doing so they pick up knowledge about software, but most important of all they are exploring a way of learning by exploring. They are acquiring **learning fluency** as well as technological fluency.

**Alan Kay**, who had a big hand in inventing most of the good things you associate with personal computers (including the name), is fond of saying that people use the word "technology" only for what was invented after they were born. That's why we don't argue about whether the piano is corrupting music with technology.

■

# Transparent and Opaque Technologies

Once upon a time it was common to be able to look inside a machine and get some idea of how it worked (or how it did not work if it was out of order). The great physicist Richard Feynmann describes, in what is certainly the best personal account ever written on masterful intuitive thinking, how much he learned as a boy from looking inside and fiddling with old-fashioned radios. There is virtually nothing of interest to be seen by looking inside a modern radio: The essential functioning happens on a microscopic scale inside black chips. In an obvious sense one can say that the old-fashioned radio was functionally **transparent**, while its modern counterpart is functionally **opaque**.

When I was a boy, cars were a transparent technology. Looking at the innards of the car and seeing how its various parts—the transmission as much as the engine—worked gave me a priceless boost in my early intellectual development. An important factor in the learning environment of those days was seeing Father open the hood, poke around and fix the car. Today it is useless even to try. The difference has to do with much more than cars.

I believe that children growing up today suffer seriously because of the opacity of the technologies around them. I therefore applaud any step towards greater transparency and deplore steps towards opacity. Most computer programs are opaque: You can't actually see the workings of the program and would probably not understand them if you could. An interesting exception is the design of Web browsers, which allows a user to see the program (albeit in an inelegant language called HTML) that was used to make that page.

Make use of this circumstance to work with your younger children on making their own Web page. It's not impossible at all. A kid really can look and see how the page was made! As for older children, they don't need their parents to help them, but I would give them a prize for turning the tables and helping a previously computer-illiterate parent build a home page for the Web.

# http://papert.www.media.mit.edu/people/papert

Six years ago that string of symbols would have had no meaning to anyone. Three years ago one percent of the American population might have recognized it as something familiar. Today perhaps ten million people have actually used, even if only in a minimal way, those strings of letters with their funny slashes and w's and periods, and almost any American who is minimally computer literate would recognize them as "something to do with the Internet."

Anyone who is *more than* minimally computer literate would recognize the string as a URL (Uniform Resource Locator), used to direct a Web browser to evoke a screen display of some sort, and would guess that this display would contain information about me. Regular users of the World Wide Web would use a strongly spatial metaphor to describe the process as *going to* or *visiting* my site, and while reading the display would talk as if they were actually there reading a page that happens to be in my computer's memory. My impression is that most would actually believe that as they read the display, their computers were somehow connected to mine.

This is a misconception if it is taken literally. A more accurate description would go something like this: The URL contains information that is used by a distant computer to send a message to my computer. The message requests a copy of a certain file, which contains a description of a page layout written in the Web's computer language, HTML. When the copy of the file arrives at the distant computer, the browser is able to construct the page layout from the HTML instructions and put it up on the distant computer's screen. In the case of a simple page with a short HTML description, the connection between the computers will have been broken long before the page is read by the owner of the distant one. If the page contains complicated graphics, a good browser will not necessarily wait until it has all been received before putting something up on the screen, so in this case the connection might *conceivably* still be in existence at the time the owner of the computer has the impression of being "in" my site. Nevertheless, the image of "being at" the far-away computer as one reads the page is highly metaphorical.

Now I am not saying that it is a harmful misconception to take the Web's standard spatial metaphor too literally. On the contrary. But I am saying that working through in one's mind a different and more literal description of the process is an exceptionally good intellectual exercise not only in developing understanding of how the digital world actually works but also in multilayered thinking.

## Frustration

Every now and then I want to throw something at my computer—or kick it or yell at it—out of sheer frustration. The worst times are when I have to wait, watching a screen passively, unable to do anything while millions of bits are trickling in through my modem or being loaded from a disk to RAM. And although computers are getting faster in their inner workings, I am finding myself having to wait more and more often. In many ways using them is getting slower.

The fact is that this technology is going out into the world in a state of marginal readiness. It does wonders. It's marvelous. But it's a mess. You'll save yourself a lot of nervous strain if you recognize this at the outset and learn enough (and trust yourself enough) to understand why.

One way to alleviate frustration at slowness is to know why it happens and whether you can be mad at someone. I don't get mad at the car industry for not letting me drive from Boston to Bangor in ten minutes because I understand about time, speed and distance for cars. When the Internet makes you wait (and wait and wait), sometimes there is a similar excuse. Often there isn't.

For example, I really needed to get into AOL to send a chapter to my editor. I was already mad at having to use AOL at all, which I did only because I had experienced problems getting AOL, which my editor uses, to receive my "file attachments" from my usual emailer. I was in a hurry but had no way to tell the system not to waste time loading graphics to make a pretty screen. So I sat twiddling my thumbs, keeping my wife waiting. . . .

I'm glad I know enough about time and speed and space in computers to know when to get mad and with whom. It calms my nerves and, besides, gives me a topic of conversation with kids who are intrigued by questions about what could have been done differently. And once in a while I can take some sort of consumerist action that might do some good.

The most common source of frustration after delays is new software that just won't run. Or worse: The software that worked until yesterday won't today. In this situation I don't get *quite* as frustrated as some people I know because I've learned to do what comes naturally to kids. When they really want to get something done they keep trying . . . and trying. But not just repetitions: They know how to vary it a little, testing the limits of the machine's stubbornness (like trying to get around a grown-up), pulling out all the tricks they remember from other times with other software.

This kid's trick is hugely valuable when all else fails and you start burning those 800 technical "support" numbers and the Net search engines. If one "helper" can't help you, try another. And don't be literal-minded in following their instructions. Like writers of manuals, they don't always say it in just the right way for you to follow exactly.

Then, of course, there are the kids. If they are at the appropriate ages, the best plan is to have them work with you. In the end if you just don't have enough time or have really run out of patience, your last resort is to leave it to them.

■

# Learning

## Learning in the Mall

Last December I went to the shopping mall in Bangor (the city nearest to where I live in rural Maine) to check out what was being offered for children in the annual present-buying season. As an experiment I imagined myself in the position of a concerned parent looking for software. Where would I go if I didn't actually know this scene? The search for an answer gave me a vivid encapsulation of today's popular **culture** of learning and computers.

With a little poking around I found a store in the mall with a sign:

### ABACUS
#### The Learning Store

Any parent who thought this might be a good place to start would have a great time browsing in a quiet atmosphere at interesting books and objects, but would have been disappointed in the quest for software. In a small space the store brought together an exceptional collection of quality materials. There were, among much else, art supplies, science kits, star charts, several interesting gadgets I had never seen before and, of course, books. Browsing around the store was in itself a model learning experience. I found myself intellectually stimulated by the profusion of good things, refreshed by the quiet, warm atmosphere and reassured by the friendly, well informed staff.

At first I was surprised, and even a little indignant, that there was no visible trace in the store of the computer presence except an IBM clone at the checkout counter. But a sense grew in me that this store was a hold-out for quality learning, and the impression was reinforced by the contrast with the next store I visited.

The biggest toy store in the region made an airplane hangar look small. Here one could not miss the prominent arrays, a hundred feet long, with signs announcing the arrival of "the latest software titles." The contrast with Abacus could not have been greater. Teeming, jostling crowds pushed shopping carts piled high with shrink-wrapped holiday gifts. No browsing here. There was no way to peep inside the CD-ROMs. I wonder if this is why they are called "titles"—does it mean that nobody really cares about the content? I certainly couldn't find an informed person who seemed able to say anything about the content of the numerous items on display.

The contrast between the two stores reflects an impression many have of the difference between "traditional learning" and "computer learning": a warm, personal human contact on one side of the divide, and a dehumanized, commodity-like atmosphere on the other. Watching, listening and asking a few questions as people in the hangar store made their selections dissipated any doubts I might have had about people having a very poor basis for decisions with serious consequences. The main criteria were fads—buy what the neighbors are talking about—and "awards."

The scene recalled the many similarities between the world of children's software and the world of Hollywood movies. The spirit of the presentation is similar, even including the software world's imitation of the Oscars. The most prestigious awards for software are the Codies, given annually by the Software Publishers Association, and the products prominently declare their status as award winners or nominees. It would be hypocritical of me to condemn this, since I was pleased enough (and you see I am even boasting about it here) when I was given a Codie (the "Lifetime Achievement Award" in 1994) and when a production (*My Make Believe Castle*) in which I participated was nominated for another (Best Children's Software). Yet even while I feel that I am part of this world, I am bothered that key decisions by parents about how and what their children learn should be strongly influenced by the results of a selection process in which media hype can win over the best thinking about learning. Marketing tactics that might be perfectly acceptable in the worlds of computer professionals and entertainers are simply wrong as influences on how children learn.

Excuse me if I am beginning to sound like a cybercritic. I do not believe that commercialism and impersonality are built into the nature of computers and computer learning. In fact I see the beginnings in the computer world of new ways in which parents who use the Internet can find the kind of warm consultation I met in the Abacus store. But the dominant trend in educational software is following a path that bothers me. The mildest criticism I can make of it is that it panders to popular prejudices about what is "educational." The more severe criticism is that most educational software powerfully reinforces the poorest sides of pre-computer education while losing the opportunity to powerfully strengthen the best sides.

Let me be specific. The education world is mired in debate about whether and how far to move "back to basics," which mostly means a rote learning approach to the three R's: reading, 'riting and 'rithmetic. What worries me is that while educators fight it out, the software industry has decided that it knows best and has put a lot more emphasis on the three R's, and especially on the rote side, than even the most conservative school policy makers have dared to go. This is especially visible in math, where the National Council of Teachers of Mathematics recently came out squarely against thinking of learning math as acquiring rote skills and number facts. I use mathematics here to illustrate a way of thinking that applies much more broadly.

Actually the educational software industry *does* know best about something, but about something other than the best ways to learn mathematics. *It has excellent knowledge about what can be most easily sold to parents.* Software that drills the kids in using numbers is easily recognized by the most uninformed parent as "math." That kind of software also happens to be easiest and least costly to produce. So it fits the surest formula for making money in the software title business: Design products that are inexpensively produced and easily marketed because they resonate with the lowest common denominator of mass-scale parental beliefs about education. This is one of many ways in which the intellectual lives of children and the educational policies of the nation (indeed the world) are increasingly being determined by business considerations. The most troubling side of the affair is that ill-founded parental beliefs are not only exploited but are reinforced in the process, a process that feeds dangerous downward spirals in educational policy.

## Design Instructions for Software to Impress the Naive Parent

Treat the child as an "answering machine": Computer asks question, child answers, computer says right or wrong. This causes naive parent to think: "learning."

Don't worry if the questions are trivial and repetitive.

—

Hold attention: Use comical graphics . . . sound effects . . . music . . . and zany responses to click on hidden hot spots. This causes some naive parents to think: "stimulation."

Others think: "Great. It kept him quiet for half an hour."

—

Don't worry about whether the effects have anything to do with what is supposed to be learned.

—

Don't feel guilty: There is no evidence anyway that even the best drill-and-practice with numbers at preschool ages will affect learning of mathematics later.

■

I do not mean to condemn the entire software industry. Some producers have concentrated on making materials that support other forms of learning, such as developing research skills, problem solving and imaginative expression. See the Resource Guide at the back of this book for some examples. But I hope that these educationally conscientious producers will not mind my inciting parents to be critical.

It's time to stand back and look at some alternatives in ways of thinking about learning. What gives me courage in doing this is knowing from experience that even parents who fall for marketing based on conventional wisdom come up with much better ideas when asked to think about their own learning. Under what conditions do you learn best? What learning was most useful to you in your life?

# Two Ways to Learn

My story of Ian and the videotape hinted at how information technology places young children in situations of choice that I never had at their age. The story of the two stores hints at a new kind of choice faced by parents. This time the choice is between philosophies of education in basic subjects. Of course the store did not offer parents a menu of theoretical principles. All that was offered was a choice of plastic containers with attractive graphics. But these containers hold much more than plastic disks. Packaged in those disks is an approach to learning math or grammar or spelling or geography or, indeed, learning about the nature of learning.

The American anthropologist Gregory Bateson expressed this best before the CD-ROM was even a glint in an inventor's eye. Every time you learn something, said Bateson, you learn two things: One is about what you thought you were learning and the other is about the method of learning used. This same idea is behind the adage often repeated by people who think that schools undermine children's desire and ability to learn independently: "The lesson best learned in school is that you can't learn without being taught." *I think we are playing with fire in risking children learning this lesson earlier.*

A parent faced with a package in the store promising to teach the three-year-old the beginnings of math may fail to appreciate the complexity of the choice. It looks simple. "Teaches math—well, that sounds pretty good. It must be better than some dumb **video game**. Can't do any harm, and maybe Johnny will grow up not hating math like I do."

Unfortunately it *can* do harm. It is harmful to plant the idea that "doing math" consists of getting a question, giving an answer and being told you are right or wrong. Learning math need not (and should not) be reduced to treating a child as "an answering machine." We can see a good example of an alternative way by recalling how we all learned one of our very first mathematical ideas.

I am going to pose what I think is a mathematical problem and then ask you two questions about it.

Put a handful of beads on the table. Imagine that you have counted them. Then spread them out in a different arrangement and ask yourself whether you would get the same number if you counted them again. "Of course," you will say, "they're the same beads. If there were seventeen before, there'll still be seventeen after. That's no problem. It's obvious."

Yes it is obvious now, but there was a time, maybe when you were four or five, when it was not at all obvious. On the contrary, it was obvious to you then that if the beads were spread out there would be more of them. Later you must somehow have learned the little "mathematical theorem" (to which the Swiss child psychologist **Jean Piaget** gave the name "the conservation of number") that says the number stays the same, is conserved, when you rearrange a bunch of things.

Here are my two questions: How do you think you first learned it, and do you think it's mathematics? Get your answer in your head before reading mine.

Of course I can't know exactly how you learned the theorem. Each person's experience is unique. But I can guess at the *kind* of learning it was. First, it is unlikely that you learned it by being told. Few adults tell children things like that and experience shows that if they do, the children usually continue to believe what they believe even if they go along with the adult view for the duration of the conversation. Most children convert to the adult opinion about conserving numbers through their own experience and their own thinking. The experience comes from living in a **culture** with a rich presence of number. Just think: Setting the table involves matching numbers; so does sharing candies with a sibling. Even the idea of one foot—one shoe—one sock brings in an early simple core of numerical thinking.

We have here a very successful kind of learning by living (and thinking) in a culture. All children succeed . . . none flunk. Nobody gets the bad feelings that come from being forced to say "I'm not good at that." Everything I know from research and intuition tells me this **home-style learning** (sometimes called "natural learning" or "Piagetian learning") is better than learning by being told, or **school-style learning**.

Home-style learning works for the conservation of number because setting tables and matching socks are "seeds" from which the idea of conservation can grow. But knowledge for which the family life does not have seeds cannot be learned in this way, which is why school-style learning becomes necessary. I believe that the computer can enrich the home culture so that in many cases in which only school-style learning was available in the past, home-style learning can now work.

It is easy to see what this means for some areas of knowledge. Ian learns more about animals in home style from National Geographic videotapes than a school would ever put in its curriculum, and although computer software for this still lags behind the videos, it will catch up and streak ahead. The case of mathematics might seem more obscure, especially if you know it only as school math.

I introduced Piaget's idea of conservation to suggest an analogy: What socks and table settings do for conservation, computer activities could do for more advanced mathematical topics. In the next section I describe a conversation with an eight-year-old which shows one way this can work—by weaving mathematical principles into something a child experiences as personal and important. I hesitated at first about including this example here because a reader might fear that it depends on my possessing esoteric mathematical knowledge. But if you think about it, you'll come to see that this "esoteric mathematics" is just common sense.

# Bits Are Bits

Descriptions of the Web use language like: A click of the mouse produces an interesting picture of a cockroach. This is true as far as it goes, but such statements fail to mention the several frustrating minutes you might wait for the picture. The issue of delays on the Internet provides an opportunity to play with some ideas about math. Why does it take the time that it takes? The superficial answer is that it's "because of graphics," but we should expect something much better from a computer-literate person.

A key step towards an answer comes from the concept of bits, which are to computational things what atoms are to material things. What is coming from the Web site are just bits. The phrase "bits are bits" is **Nicholas Negroponte**'s way of emphasizing that hardware involved in downloading does not know whether these bits will produce a picture or a sound or a piece of text or a computer program. You may have to read his book *Being Digital* or his column in *Wired* to appreciate why this is one of those facts that may seem too obvious to mention but really represents a momentous turning point in intellectual history. Meantime, let's go back to the numbers, which I'll discuss by describing a session with an eight-year-old.

When I said to him, find a number just to start the ball rolling in our quest for answers, his instinct was to choose the modem's speed—14.4, which means 14,400 bits per second. Since we were wanting to know why the picture took a minute (not a second, not an hour) to appear on the screen, it seemed natural to ask: How many bits are passed in this minute? Following an urge to avoid calculations that are uselessly precise, we decided to take 14,400 x 60 as "about a million bits per minute." We then went on to ask: Does a picture need something like a million bits? And if so, why?

We knew that pictures were made of pixels, and the pixels were made of bits. So next we asked: How many pixels to a picture, and how many bits to a pixel? A magnifying glass enabled us to see the pixels on our laptop screen. We counted the number in an inch and calculated from that that our picture was made of about 100,000 pixels. Now the chase was heating up. This picture took about a minute to download; that means about a million bits. The picture has 100,000 pixels, so if a pixel consisted of about ten bits, everything would work out. We would have our explanation! But *does* a pixel consist of about ten bits? My eight-year-old showed me an advertisement for a monitor that claimed "8 bit color" and reminded me that for our purposes, eight was as good as ten. We had our answer.

He happened to know also from "fooling around" (as he put it) that his computer had 256 colors. We could have pursued a discussion of how a bit was like a switch (on or off) and how you could make 256 patterns with eight switches. But my friend wanted to get back to surfing, so I called it a day and will wait for another chance.

This account leaves a lot of loose ends. For example, if the computer wasn't a laptop, we couldn't have counted pixels. In that case we might have "fooled around" until we found the computer's screen resolution. Also, some people will notice that we ignored "compression." But this incompleteness only strengthens my main point, which is that by playing with math in an incomplete and approximate way, we were still able to make progress towards resolving a puzzle.

# Constructivism

I don't believe that my parents gave two thoughts to the teaching of mathematics. That wasn't their business. That would happen at school, and professional teachers would know how to do it. This nonchalance was not because they sloughed off all responsibility for their children's learning. On the contrary, in retrospect I believe they gave me very good conditions for learning. But in those days there was no reason for parents to think much about teaching math. The part of math that could be learned in the home style was learned so well that it was not even recognized as something that needed learning, and for the rest of math there was no serious alternative to leaving it to the schools.

The well-established division between home-style and school-style learning was not challenged until the computer did so. Since this division was imposed (on the whole) by conditions of life, parents did not have to connect it with a large-scale theoretical debate that has grown up in the world of professional educators about whether greater efforts should be made to shift the learning in schools closer to what has traditionally been done in the preschool years at home. Under the name **construc-tivism**, this theoretical movement argues that learning happens best when it is self-directed. It complains that much traditional teaching is based on a model of a pipeline through which knowledge passes from teacher to student. The name constructivism derives from an alternative model, according to which the learner has to *construct* knowledge afresh every time. Piaget, the most influential advocate of constructivist education, popularized the slogan: "To understand is to invent." The role of the teacher is to create the conditions for invention rather than to provide ready-made knowledge.

The Greek historian Xenephon formulated in the context of training horses a precept that is still often ignored in teaching children. Nothing forced, he said, is beautiful; if you want a horse to make beautiful movements you must make sure that the animal wants to do them. The history of more modern writing about horses is peppered with allusions to this idea, stated in opposition to what came to be known in the twentieth century as *behaviorism*: the idea that the way to train a horse (or a rat or even a person) to perform a complex behavior is to break it up into pieces that may not be beautiful in themselves but which fit together in the end like a puzzle that is supposed to give rise to the magnificent final result. For the behaviorist, the final result has to be known only by the trainer-teacher. It has no meaning for the trainee-student. Many practitioners of the art of dressage, in which horses and riders move together in movements of breathtaking elegance, believe, on the contrary, that the horse should always be shown the result you want.

I think Xenephon would have liked the story of Jenny. The curriculum designers thought the way to teach grammar was by carving it into such small "learning bites" that each could be memorized, practiced and tested. But the bites were so small that Jenny never saw the whole picture and never saw any reason to want to make it. Her computer experience enabled her to find the very beautiful and very **powerful idea** that lies behind grammar.

**Neil Postman**, one of the sharpest critics of foolishness in education and the media and author of *Teaching as a Subversive Activity* and *Amusing Ourselves To Death*, takes from the philosopher the precept "He who has a *why* to live can bear with almost any *how*" and turns it into a principle for educators: For a student who has a why to learn, almost any how will serve.

In that spirit, I have explored in my research the idea of creating a learning environment in which there is no direct teaching at all. But in the practical world, especially when one is giving advice to other people, caution is obligatory. So my position here recognizes the reality of both kinds of learning—constructivist and instructionist—and concentrates on the balance between them. In fact my strongest advice to parents is to experiment cautiously with a shift in the balance. Nevertheless my sense of greatest danger from the rash use of computers is that they swing a balance heavily towards instructionism.

# Make a Video Game

Few people who care about children's learning can fail to be envious of the enormous energy and concentration evoked by **video games**. "If only that energy could be mobilized for something important like____" (where you fill in the particular interest of the individual educator). Let's look at three ways to make this wish come true.

### The Instructionist Approach: Make a game teach.

This one is overwhelmingly the most commonly followed by software makers. The reasoning is simple. Children like to play the games. We like them to learn the multiplication tables. So let's make a game in which players have to give the correct answer to a little multiplication problem before proceeding. This can be characterized as trying to achieve **school-style learning** in the context of a game.

### The Constructionist Approach: Make a game yourself.

Who me? My kids? We're not brains! We don't know about computers! In Chapter 6 we will take a short tour of computer game-making that will dissipate any skepticism you may have that children can make their own games. The experience will also give you a concrete image of how much they can learn by doing so and show you that this kind of experience is accessible to children at all ages going down at least to age five and can be challenging to people of all ages going up indefinitely.

What will children learn by making a game? They will learn some technical things, for example to program computers. They will learn some knowledge traditionally incorporated in the school curriculum, for example in order to make shapes and program movements they will have to think about geometry and about numbers. They will develop some psychological, social and moral kinds of thinking.

Most important of all in my view is that children will develop their sense of self and of control. For instance, they will begin to learn what it's like to control their own intellectual activity. Most instructionist software resembles games in casting the child in a reactive role. The machine asks a question. The kid responds. The machine creates a threat in the game. The kid responds. By some sleight of language this is called interactive—as if the two sides, human and machine, were in a relationship of equality. To my mind the position of the child here is, in the most essential respects, basically passive.

A second way that game-making can help develop a sense of self is by counteracting the cultural pressure to think of technology as something "other people" can understand and make. I do not want to see a generation of children grow up to be people for whom anything technological is an unintelligible black box. *If you use a computer game you should know how to make one.* I do not expect all children to want to devote their lives to understanding every piece of technology that comes their way. But I want them to know that they can if they wish to. I consider it to be fundamentally anti-educational to adopt a black-box, it's-beyond-me attitude to the most pervasive technology of our times.

The question is: Will the child program the computer or will the computer program the child?

Will the child run the machine or will the machine run the child?

■

My experience with children making games shows that a large proportion find this exciting; games are important to them, so making one gives them a sense of doing something important. It also gives them an opportunity to develop their thinking about how people are different from one another. Few people will engage in making a game without caring about whether others will want to play it. So the young game-maker feels a need to think about the audience, to construct the game to be psychologically right as well as technically right. And this connects to the third approach I shall mention here.

## The Learning-about-Learning Approach

This approach calls into question the envious educator's assumption that games are good for learning only when they can be directly related to school-style knowledge.

I have asked a number of children to teach me how to play their favorite video games. More than one at some point impatiently made a remark like "You can't learn like that" and followed this by giving me some very sensible advice about how to go about learning. Timothy Gallwey, the author of a series of books with titles such as *The Inner Game of Tennis*, became famous for advising players to let themselves go as they played and keep their self-conscious thinking (and embarrassments) for before or after. Children have given me essentially the same advice and shown that they knew how to follow it too.

We are seeing here a new interest aroused in children by playing these games. It is easy to see why. Millions of kids have a strong interest in being the first on the block to master the latest game. That means having an interest in learning something as fast and as well as possible. And *that* means having an interest in thinking about learning. How different from school, where very few children think about how to learn. That is the job of the teacher. The job of the kid is to do what the teacher says.

In summary I review the three approaches with a brief statement of what parents can do about them:

| APPROACH | ACTION |
|---|---|
| Instructing Games | Be skeptical. An honest teaching program is better, though both share the weakness of placing the learner in a reactive stance. |
| Constructing Games | Obtain suitable software. If possible learn how to use it yourself. |

| Learning about Learning | Engage in conversations with the children about strategies for learning. To keep it concrete, learn some games under their tutelage. Extend the same idea to discussing "strategy" as a **powerful idea**. Make a family game out of collecting strategies for all sorts of activities. |

# Bad Software

With a positive example in front of us, I switch to the other side now and set out what I see as the most objectionable features of the educational software **culture** developing around us. The first of these we have already discussed:

### FIRST OBJECTIONABLE FEATURE:
### It gives agency to the machine, not to the child.

This is the question of who runs whom: the machine or the child. Like all the features I shall mention, this is of course not confined to computers. It is part of our culture that we think of children as "answering machines"—hoping to instruct them by putting questions to them and correcting the answers given. Instead I want to see children retain control of their intellectual process, developing their innate instincts to pose and pursue their own questions.

### SECOND OBJECTIONABLE FEATURE:
### It is deceptive and proud of it.

I have seen many dozens of advertisements for software that make promises like:

### Such Fun Your Child Won't Know She Is Learning

I am horrified by the message. The suggestion is that learning is a nasty pill that must be sugarcoated with fun and games. It is true that learning has sometimes been given a bad name by poor practices in school and even by some parents whose constant refrain is "Do your learning. You can have fun afterwards." But one of the great things the computer can do is turn this around and restore the kind of enjoyment of learning you see if you watch an infant— or a scientist. Both are learning all the time and they know it and they love it.

Flip through a computer magazine and you'll find many variants on the same theme:

### She'll Have Such Fun She Won't Know It's Math.

If you hated school math as much as most people you might have a lot of sympathy with this one. But I don't have one bit of sympathy. I hated math in school but went on to become a professor of mathematics at a prestigious university. This didn't happen to me by people disguising math as something else so I wouldn't notice I was getting it. I would never have fallen in love with it that way. What actually happened was exactly the opposite. I realized one day that something I really liked was really math.

I am not suggesting that all parents should hope their children will become professors of mathematics. I am sure that many would hate the idea. But I do think that whatever level of mathematics a person aspires to do, it will be better done consciously and knowingly than through subterfuge. The goal of a parent or teacher must not be to slip some mathematics unnoticed into a kid's intellectual diet but to find mathematics that a kid will love to do. Maybe this math won't be fractions. That's fine. Kids who get to love any kind of math can use that as a stepping stone to doing any other kind. Those who hate it all will gain nothing by being programmed to give the right answer.

The best learning is learning that is embraced and enjoyed. Children love to learn until they are taught otherwise. Indeed even then, while most people may hate being taught, I believe that everyone, especially every child, always likes learning.

I can almost hear some parents saying: *"I just wish that were right; I wish my children were like that, but I think they really need their learning pills sugared."*

Of course you know your children and I don't. But I would be immensely surprised if they really disliked learning. If they do, this is not something born in them; it is something that was done to them, and this is a case where what is done *can* be undone.

Below you will find a learning story about some children who had been learning something new—in fact an elementary form of programming—that they considered hard and yet loved learning. If you have trouble imagining your children in this situation, I suggest that you keep your eyes and ears open for a few days for situations in which your children seem to believe that hard is good. I think you will find some and that they will often involve learning. Listen also to the nuances of what your school-age children say about school and homework. There is a prevalent tendency to think that when children under-perform at school and dislike schoolwork this is because it is too hard. Nothing could be more wrong. Most dislike of school work comes from finding it boring, the exact opposite of finding it too difficult. *Children, like everyone else, don't want "easy"—they want "challenging" and "interesting"—and this implies "hard."*

Many parents do not give their children the respect of considering that if they don't like school work it may be the school work that is to blame.

■

A LEARNING STORY

# Hard Fun

One of the best formulations of a fundamental principle of learning came from a conversation reported to me by Carol Sperry, the director of a pioneering computers-in-schools project supported by **IBM** and the Silicon Valley Technology Center at the Gardner Academy in San Jose, California.

One kindergarten section was waiting to take the place of another section that had just had its first encounter with the computers. A student recognized a friend coming out of the room and asked: "What was it like?" The friend replied: "It was fun." Then paused and added: "It was really hard."

The relation between "fun" and "hard" may need some interpretation. Did this mean "it was fun in spite of being hard" or "it was fun because it was hard"? The teacher who heard the tone of the conversation and knew the children had no doubt. The child meant it was "fun" because it was "hard." It was "hard" and this made it all the more "fun." Since then I have listened to children with an ear sensitized by this experience and have come to know that the concept of **hard fun** is widely present in children's thinking.

---

## THIRD OBJECTIONABLE FEATURE:
### It favors quick reactions over long-term thinking.

This feature is often cited as what is wrong with video games. But it is equally present in most of the problem/answer kinds of software. By contrast think about a long-term project such as making a game. In the course of doing this the child-constructor will encounter numerous problems. Some of them will be solved. Some of them will be dissolved. Some will be bypassed by finding another way that avoids the problem.

The third objectionable feature is frequently stated as if it were a great virtue in the form:

### The Software Provides Immediate Feedback.

Of course it is important to see the results of your actions, but this does not have to take the form of a right/wrong comment. A different sense of "feedback" is shown by the next learning story.

# Ian Finds a Castle on the Screen

Ian was five when I gave him the CD-ROM of *My Make Believe Castle*. His mother reports that in the forty-eight waking hours after the CD first ran, Ian was preoccupied with it for close to forty.

*My Make Believe Castle* is a **microworld**, a little world of things that live and perform actions on a computer screen. There is a castle with a moat outside, rooms inside, furniture and other objects in the rooms. There are characters appropriate to the image of a medieval castle: a knight, a princess, a witch, a dragon, a horse.

What makes this a very special microworld for children of four or five or six is the degree of control they can exercise to create amusing and sometimes action scenarios. They do this by what is in fact a very simple form of programming. Try it on the CD-ROM.

The child works by placing little action icons on the screen. When a character touches one of these it performs a version of the action; for example it might leap, or turn, or break into a run or become angry. So by laying out icons, interesting sequences of actions can be programmed. The icons can then be made invisible so that the actions play out as if by the will of the characters.

I watched a five-year-old try to set things up so that two characters would start in different places, meet after wandering for a while and then walk off together. Doing this involved quite a complex feat of coordination and visualization. The child had to solve a series of problems, each of which brought the goal closer. Although it took time and although at all intermediate stages it was clear to an adult onlooker who knew the material that the child was missing something essential, it was never necessary to say (or even think) "you are wrong." Instead one could see the positive and be able to say (or just think) honestly and respectfully, "yes that's right, keep going, you'll get it."

---

Sometimes I wonder whether a kid's "short attention span" means just the opposite: a very long attention span for what the kid is really thinking about.

Not just a kid. Me too. Imagine this. I am thinking about *machipajo*. You come along and ask me to watch the kettle. I do it for a few minutes and then my mind has wandered back to what interested me. Does this mean I have a *short attention span* (for kettles) or a *long attention span* (for *machipajo*)?

■

---

## Principles for Choosing Software

■ *Is the toy running the child or is the child running the toy?* Look for software that allows the learner to take charge of self-directed exploration, construction and creation.

■ *Is there room for fantasy, make-believe and imagination as well as facts and skills?* Imagination is in the driver's seat of all creative activity—making a discovery, starting a business, developing ambition, choosing a gift . . . anything you can imagine. Look for software that allows hard thinking and the learning of facts to be practiced and strengthened while building make-believe worlds.

■ *Is there something to share?* Look for software that allows a child to make something that can be shared with you or others: a picture, an animated cartoon, a birthday card. Look for software that allows genuine collaboration that you and the child can both enjoy. Look for software that allows activity that you and the child can talk about, and then talk about it in a way that reinforces the child's pride of ownership but also adds a little.

- *Try it before you buy it.* Look for software with many layers. If after five minutes you can't understand *anything* about what's going on, that's bad. But if you can understand *everything* in five minutes, that's far worse. The software is too superficial. Look for software that *you* find interesting. Remember that the best literature for children is good literature for anyone.

- *Look for a balanced mental diet.* There is no such thing as the single best food for the mind or for the body. But just as we recognize the need to balance kinds of foods such as proteins, fats, and carbohydrates, we can also balance components of a mental diet. Structure comes from understanding **powerful ideas**. Facts are important, but taken alone are empty learning, like empty calories. Energy comes from interests and fantasies.

■

# Microworlds and Hyperworlds

I am at an age where I can look back on fifty years of the computer's development.

The first "computer" I ever had was one that I made myself when I was a student in the 1940s. It couldn't do anything useful: It took longer to feed a problem into the machine (by setting switches) than to find the answer in one's own head. What was interesting (and "educational" for me) was inventing and building the machine rather than using it. Sometimes I wonder about how the quality of my learning experience compares with those of modern kids whose parents buy them ready-made machines about a hundred million times as powerful as the one I made! Such ruminations are responsible for my development of the idea of **microworlds,** where the big powerful machine is used as a medium for making simple, restricted worlds. In these worlds, learning can take place without being hampered by the complexities of the real world. It sounds perverse but in fact making something out of "bits" (software) has advantages over making things out of "atoms" such as pieces of metal and wood and plastic.

The first "real computer" I programmed (in the late fifties) fitted what has now become the familiar story of computers following the evolution towards smaller, cheaper and more powerful. To say that the machine was as big as a barn is misleading—it was bigger than many barns. Unlike my homebuilt machine it could do useful work, though far less than the laptop I carry in my briefcase today. Compared with modern machines it was "unconnected" in a number of ways. Today we are accustomed to having a computer that sits in a study or an office and so becomes part of our life. Using the ACE (as it was called) was a big production: one had to schedule "computer time" well in advance, punch out a program on cards and carry them over to where the machine sat like a great pagan temple. There wasn't even the minimal kind of connection with other people and other machines that was to come in the wake of shared programming languages. Everything about this machine was isolated and idiosyncratic.

Things changed fast. By the middle sixties I could work on a computer from my home or office. The computer was somewhere else, but I could have a "terminal" that looked rather like a modern personal computer connected by telephone to a big expensive machine. Two ideas made this possible: the technology of telecommunication and especially an idea called time-sharing. Sitting at my home terminal I could get the impression that I was controlling the computer, at least as long as I did not ask it to do anything complicated. In fact many other people had the same illusion. The computer was actually giving each user a small fraction of a second of its time during which it would check whether anything had been typed in, take any needed action and send out information to go up on the user's screen. Then on to the next use. Most often, if one was doing something like word processing that was not much strain on the computer, it would be back again before one had noticed its absence.

In the seventies it seemed like a great step forward to have one's own personal computer. No telephone lines were needed. No sharing of computer time with other people. On the other hand it was isolating: I missed checking who else was using the machine and perhaps passing a message or sharing a document or a program. However, the idea of connecting computers was spreading in a development that would culminate in the modern Internet. The new technology would combine the advantages of powerful self-contained personal computers with even more connectivity than we knew in the time-sharing days.

In a sense, many millions of computers all over the world can now be merged into one huge computer. When I get to the end of this chapter I'll click on a few buttons and the text will be transmitted to my editor, who is more than a thousand miles from here. Even that is old-fashioned. Yesterday I read a paper written by one of my students by connecting (again by a very simple action) my computer directly to his computer and reading the paper as if it were stored in the hard drive of my own machine. The only action the student had taken to make this possible was "telling" his computer many months ago that I had permission to "get into it" and read files.

The children in the learning story about yucky creatures were doing something very similar. Using a software tool called a Web browser, they were able to use a distant computer in some respects as if it were their own. I find it valuable to divide the consequences of this potential into two groups (although in reality they can be mixed, matched and merged).

One way to use the Internet is to get access to software that will be used just as if one had bought it on a CD-ROM and loaded it into one's own computer. The software could be a game or it could be the tools for making a game. The software might be used by "downloading" it to one's own computer or (at present less commonly) by running it on another computer under control of one's own. This kind of use might cost less and take less time than buying the CD-ROM, but in principle the kinds of activities it permits are almost the same.

The second way, which is captured by the metaphor of "surfing," introduces something very new. The children in the Yucky story "visited" several dozen computers and did so without any preformed plan—what they saw at each site suggested where they might go next. Children who do this a lot might peep into thousands of computers in every country of the world. The key element here is not the learning advantages of working in an individual microworld; it is opening a larger "hyperworld" in which the microworlds are mere atoms.

# Two Kinds of Knowing

The guiding image of the **microworld** is a "world" limited enough to be thoroughly explored and completely understood. It is the right kind of place to learn to use knowledge that requires deep mastery. In an analogy between ideas and people, microworlds are the worlds of people we know intimately and well.

There is also another kind of knowing: knowing casually. Some ideas and facts are acquaintances rather than intimates. This is a world of looser connections, like the people one meets at cocktail parties—a ten-minute conversation and then off to the next. The people we treat in this way are not necessarily less interesting or less worth knowing. In fact every now and then a party encounter will blossom into a deep friendship. But we all have limited energy, time and capacity to establish deep relationships, whether with people or with ideas. We need shallower ones as well.

Hyperworlds are large worlds of these loose connections. The ultimate hyperworld is the World Wide Web—that great, exciting and frustrating province of cyberspace. The ultimate in hyperworldly activity is surfing the Web: jumping through easy connections from one "site" to another.

A child working with *My Make Believe Castle*, or arranging dolls into a family or building with **Lego** experiments many times with the same limited number of elements until they are thoroughly well known. A challenging activity such as making a **video game** is likely to have a few focal problems, such as coordinating the moves, that can be made by a central character. This is work that is obviously hard and perhaps, for someone who is not immersed in it, less obviously fun. But what about surfing the Web? Is this hard too, or just fun?

I do not try here to impose a value system that places one kind of world or one way of knowing ahead of the other. We need both. Like diet for the body, diet for the mind requires balance. The perfect single nutrient does not and cannot exist.

The idea of balance between two kinds of knowledge is illuminated by looking at familiar caricatural versions of people with opposite imbalances: The extreme *hyperknowers* will always beat you at trivial pursuits; they know a little about everything—"jack of all trades, master of none." On the other side, the extreme *microknowers* invite the classic remark about knowing more and more about less and less until they know everything about nothing. Both kinds of unbalanced knowers have erudition in their own ways, but both come out sounding plain silly in situations requiring good common sense and judgment.

The value of surfing depends on how it is integrated into other activities. The positive side is the opportunity to follow personal interests and the excitement of the chase in acquiring knowledge. I see it as analogous to the kind of browsing in dictionaries and encyclopedias I loved to do as a kid when time was freer and still do now when I can. I usually go to the dictionary to look up a particular word. But quite often after I have done this another word on the page (or perhaps something in the definition I have just read) captures my interest and so starts a process from which I might wake up several hours later! Believers in discipline might see this as wasteful. But I know that interests and knowledge that started in this way have played a significant role in my intellectual life. I am sure that surfing on the Net has the potential to bring similar and greater benefits.

The negative side becomes serious only if the excitement of surfing becomes the dominant model for relating to knowledge. I have criticized school severely for being too directive, but there is also an obvious danger of developing a "grasshopper" approach to intellectual activities. What can a parent do to maximize the benefit and minimize the danger?

Ultimately the problem facing all parents and educators is helping learners maintain balance. This is not any easier in the case of mental than in the case of bodily diets. In fact it is harder, since there is an even stronger reason here to value individual preferences that preclude universal prescriptions.

The difficulties inherent in establishing and maintaining good balance in mental diet are compounded by commercial practices analogous to selling highly sweetened cereals that not only appeal to children now but manipulate the development of their taste in the future. I am sure that when we eventually understand better than anyone does today the principles of good "mental nutrition," we will look back and see trends in children's software development in the same light as many parents now see the self-serving development of a child's sweet tooth by the overuse of sugar in certain food products.

Many children will by natural inclination as well as by acquired habit find one kind of knowing especially attractive. My approach is not to try to keep children away from the activity that threatens the balance, but to think about how to blend more mental nutrients into it.

If the Web is the ultimate hyperworld, the ultimate **microworld** is programming, and programming by children is almost synonymous with the language **Logo**, which I initiated in 1965.

Logo was guided by the learning aphorism "no threshold, no ceiling." Most natural languages are like that. English is learnable because it has the part we call baby talk, so that infants can begin using it, but it can also serve the purposes of poets and philosophers. Logo is a language for instructing computers so designed that children are able within a few minutes to make the computer do something they want. The second half of the aphorism requires Logo to be a full-fledged, universal programming language—anything that can be programmed at all can be programmed in Logo.

Two other ideas guided the design: I believed that children would joyously learn to program if given a chance, and that programming would enhance their learning of everything else.

Around 1980 this idea was brought to educators by my book *Mindstorms: Children, Computers and Powerful Ideas* and by commercial publication of Logo. The response was encouraging. Hundreds of thousands of teachers read *Mindstorms* and tens of thousands of schools adopted Logo.

Today Logo is represented in schools by a community of Logo teachers dedicated to exploring new ways of learning despite absurdly limited computer access and despite the immune reaction evoked in most schools by the beginnings of serious change. Although perhaps half the schools who ever used Logo have dropped it for easier and more conservative uses of computers, I see an incipient shift of interest in schools from computer literacy back to **technological fluency**. The new trends are well served by the newest Logo (called **MicroWorlds**), which has lowered its threshold and raised its ceiling by taking advantage of new ideas and faster computers (see this book's CD-ROM).

# Values

## What's Important

Recent discussion in the public forum about education in the United States has given a great deal of attention to the teaching of ethical, spiritual and religious values. People take passionate stands on questions such as: Should values be taught by schools or by parents? Should there be courses in schools on moral questions? But in all this discussion virtually no attention is paid to a far more important set of issues about values inherent in the way that education is conducted. If the practices of educators are seen by students as deceptive, it hardly matters what they say.

The story about how Jenny learned grammar touched a number of issues. Some of these receive their share of attention in current discussions about the theory of learning and the practice of education. For example, there is growing acceptance of the idea that what children learn should be "meaningful." One issue that has received far too *little* attention is implicit in Jenny's statement that she did not believe her teachers.

Jenny had failed to see why she should learn grammar. When asked about this, she came close to saying that she just did not believe the explanations given by teachers about the need for learning grammar. She thought, as most savvy students do, that teachers are told what to teach. They don't teach grammar (or fractions or whatever) out of conviction that this is good for the students. Thus the education system fosters a cynical impression among students such as Jenny that "teachers lie," even though the particular teachers involved in her case might have been the most upright and fanatically honest in the world.

Many teachers work hard to create a more trusting relationship with their students, and later in the book I shall have something to say about how you can support these teachers in your children's schools. For the moment, the issue is not what teachers do but what *you* do. My recommendation is that the highest priority in thinking about learning in your family should be devoted to upholding the values of **honesty** and respect for individuals.

This is not always easy to do. I believe, however, that you can create conditions in the spirit of what worked for Jenny, provided that you make the effort to learn to take control of the computer rather than rely on ready-made activities. You will certainly have to stand up against some powerful trends in the public **computer culture**. And you may have to take a stand against the policies of your children's schools.

I would emphasize three "values issues" closely related to learning, and then a fourth that requires very special attention:

■ Honesty and deception

■ Respect

■ Materialism

■ Relationships on the Internet

# Honesty and Deception in Learning

**Deception** in teaching and learning is in essential contradiction with the goals of moral education. Telling people that lying is bad when you know that you lie to them is not only morally indefensible but also guaranteed to produce the opposite of the desired result. Kids will do as you do before they do as you say—and if they don't they ought to. And they will learn to be cynical about it as well.

It is certainly very hard, and perhaps impossible, to justify the teaching of a lot of what is in the school curriculum. In many cases where I can justify it, I do not know how to do so in terms that will be meaningful to most elementary-aged students, let alone preschool children. Grammar is one of those things. But there is a lot more as well, including most of the stuff taught in math classes.

Fortunately I don't have to say what teachers could have done to justify what they taught in the days before computers. Today I can ask them to look at Jenny and others we shall be meeting as models of what can be done.

*A principal connection between the computer and moral development comes via the computer's ability to provide a context in which knowledge is seen as having an understandable purpose and meaning, thus removing the need to lie about it.* Given this, it is doubly bizarre that "educational software" most often continues to follow the old patterns, reinforcing the deception instead of making it unnecessary.

# Respect in Learning

I sometimes play chess with my grandsons. I expect that in a couple of years one of them is going to be able to beat me consistently. But in the meantime my chess experience puts me in a position in which I can always win. As an adult I would not mind playing with a master player who would always beat me. In fact I would enjoy it as a learning experience or just for the pleasure of having a participant's close-up view of very good chess. But at age six I might have found it frustrating to know that I would lose every time.

One solution is to allow the child to win by making deliberate blunders. Although I have sometimes resorted to doing this, I think it is disrespectful and don't like it. Fortunately in chess there are traditional methods of dealing with the problem, for example by playing with a handicap—a concept well known in the **culture of children** in the form of giving a smaller child a "start" in a race. In chess one can give the opponent an advantage by playing without one or more pieces, or one can play with a clock, cutting down the permitted time for thinking to compensate for being a stronger player.

Another way to give young learners the advantage of playing against serious opposition without depriving them of the pleasure of winning is to buy a chess-playing program whose level of performance can be adjusted to match the child's. This helps, and I would recommend it, but it is not a full answer because playing chess is not a purely logical activity. It would be sad to play chess and forgo the social aspects of the game.

In practice a mix of all these strategies, including an occasional straight unhandicapped game, copes well enough with the problem of developing a respectful attitude to a child's chess playing. The challenge is harder to meet when we leave the limited world of chess and step into the larger world of learning how things work.

This challenge is illustrated by the results of an investigation by **Jean Piaget**, in which the eminent scientist-philosopher-psychologist asked children, "What makes the wind?"

If you don't already know what he found, stop for a moment to think about how you think a child of four or five might answer. To do this you have to try to put out of your mind all that knowledge you have accumulated about movements of huge blocks of air and all those images of swirling clouds you picked up from the weather channel or the evening news. You also have to put out of your mind the idea of finding one answer to a question. Think of three or four explanations that children might offer. What do you think the children said?

I have asked many children Piaget's question and followed up whatever they said with a discussion about how they knew and what they would say to someone who did not think so. Of course not all children gave the same answer. But most of them gave an answer that has much in common with the kinds of answers Piaget heard most frequently: The trees make the wind by waving their branches. The clouds make the wind by pushing the air.

In their discussion of how they knew, some children of five and even less showed quite impressive sophistication. For example one waved a hand near my face, saying "Do you feel that?" and when I said that I did, went on to point out that if a little hand could make wind, just think how much wind a tree could make waving its huge branches. And what a lot of trees there are! No wonder wind can be so strong.

Now in my view there is very good thinking in this, however much it conflicts with meteorological orthodoxy. Nor is this good thinking a rare kind of occurrence. Every parent who pays attention can tell you interesting theories their children came up with. And they feel proud too! Where there are differences among parents is in what they do about it. Many parents and almost all teachers feel impelled to put the kid right.

I see a real conflict in this situation. On the one hand, as parents or teachers we have a duty to help children develop their understanding of the world and their skill at finding explanations. After all we can't have children growing up believing any old thing. We have to educate them! If you don't tell them they are wrong they will never get to do better.

On the other hand, we want to encourage children to think for themselves rather than simply echo what they are told. We want to be able to show respect for them as thinkers and theory makers. Yet we can be sure that their own theories are not likely to be exactly the ones that generations of scientists have developed, and the scenario of "giving feedback" will always end up with "Wonderful theory, Johnny. Good try. But now I'll tell you the real truth." Frankly I'd give up trying. And most kids eventually do. Or keep their theories to themselves.

This is a genuine dilemma. There is no doubt that children's thinking can't just be allowed to run wild. On the other hand there is no doubt that putting them right all the time will inhibit the development of their capacity to think for themselves.

---

The scandal of education is that every time you teach something you deprive a child of the pleasure and benefit of discovery.

■

# The Constructionist Solution

An answer to the dilemma is suggested by looking back at the first years of a child's life, when a volcano of learning takes place with nobody "putting the kid right" or "telling the real explanation." Why doesn't the learning of these toddlers run wild? Although they do come to hold beliefs in words or in actions that will have to be revised later, their learning is quite obviously adaptive. How does this happen?

The answer is obvious. It is because the learning is action-oriented and gets its feedback not from the yes-no of adult authority but from the resistance and the guidance of reality. Some attempted actions do not produce the expected results. Some produce surprising results. The child comes to learn that it is not sufficient to want a result for it to happen. One must act in an appropriate way, and "appropriate" means based on understanding.

A great deal of learning happens in this way, without any deliberate intervention by adults. I don't mean that this learning would
happen without adults and without living in a world made by
adults. Children learn to speak English (or Chinese) because the
people around them speak English (or Chinese). Children learn to
think in quantities because they live in a world so constructed that
quantities are important. But then what can we do to improve the
way in which the world facilitates learning?

A common view (which I've called instructionism) is that the best
way for this to happen is to have more instruction: Spend more
time telling kids what you think they ought to know. The idea that
you should *stimulate* kids is very similar. The instructionist thinks
in terms of *doing something to the child.*

I have talked already about how making a **video game** can lead a
child to new learning. Here nobody "does anything to the child."
Somebody creates a situation in which it is the child who does
something. So we enhance learning by enriching the child's environment—by providing a new kind of material out of which something can be made. The video game is made out of software, or
bits, just as a piece of furniture is made out of wood, or atoms.

Of course we did not have to wait for the computer in order for
children to learn by constructing or even for adults to enhance
the process by providing new construction materials. The development of "construction sets" has a long history of doing just
that. Once upon a time children built structures with sticks and
stones and mud and whatever they found. Later they built with
objects such as wooden blocks that were invented and made for
this purpose. Building and knocking down towers of blocks is a
learning-rich activity. Modern materials make it more so. I have
been especially associated in my work with **Lego** because I think
it has some special features as a construction material. Using it
leads to learning a lot about what makes structures strong. A less
obvious idea that might be inspired by Lego is that a few kinds
of elements can be used to construct an infinite variety of dif-

ferent composed objects. I am sure that if you think about it, or better still spend some time building with Lego yourself, you will construct your own list of what can be learned—much better than reading my list.

We did not have to wait for the computer to have a construction set. But we did have to wait for it in order to have an *inexhaustible* construction set. This it provides, and in doing so offers us a very clear example of doing something that will enhance learning but that is not in any sense "instruction" and does not risk eroding the child's sense of self and self-confidence as we "teach the truth."

In my discussion of Ian and the tape I noted that the Garden of Eden of early learning runs out as the child exhausts the possibilities of the immediately reachable world. The moral of the tape story was that technology could give Ian access to a wider world of knowledge. However it can do more than this: Technology can also give access to a wider world of *action*. So by doing a wider range of actions the child can obtain an immensely wider range of feedback from the world. This then is the opportunity to broaden learning without running into the paradox inherent in relying on adult judgment.

# Valuing People

"YOU RETARD." "YOU'RE DUMB." . . . The idea of valuing people by some impression of their supposed mental capacities is well entrenched in **children's culture**.

This way of valuing people is encouraged by school's ways of thinking. Take math once more as an example. People put on a show of not being ashamed—or even of being proud—to think of themselves in terms such as "don't have a head for figures." Each student is defined as a bundle of aptitudes and ineptitudes. The reason is that school provides such constricted ways of doing each thing, especially math, that it matches only some students' intellectual **styles**. The computer provides opportunities to do math in many ways and as part of many personal interests. Most people who think they cannot do math were simply put off by the way they were made to do it.

It is widely believed that some people just can't do math. The argument for this belief is incredibly weak and is mostly based on the observation that many people do not learn to do math very well at school. Before you accept this argument consider the following:

Most people who learn French at school learn it very badly. They emerge speaking French as badly as most people do math. But can we honestly say that these people do not have "a head for French"? Surely not. We know quite well that if they grew up in France they would speak French as fluently as the French. If they lack any aptitude it can't be the aptitude for speaking French. It must be the aptitude for learning French in the particularly unfavorable conditions provided by our classrooms.

But why not say the same about math? Perhaps all those who seem not to have a head for math really could do it perfectly well if they grew up in **Mathland**.

*Mathland is to math what France is to French . . .*

By using the computer as a math-speaking entity we can in fact make a Mathland, which is a place where mathematics can be learned not only effectively but honestly and respectfully. We have some examples in this book: children learning fractions by making software to teach about fractions, children facing mathematical problems of shape and movement in creating a video game. Even as they surf the Internet, they use mathematics in thinking about the time needed to transfer files.

# Materialism

The very idea of a computer for the kids is intertwined with a growing materialism in the lives of children. As the ultimate expensive gift, it comes as the apex of a movement towards more and more expensive toys that is fraught with danger for the development of social and personal values in children and perhaps even for their development as learners.

I see this contradiction as a dilemma to be resolved rather than even the flimsiest reason to deprive children of the best possible computer experience. There is no question in my mind that every home should have a computer, and when the family can afford to do so there should be an additional computer for the children. Indeed in most cases I would give children the priority over their parents in access to the computer. But the dilemma of how to think about this needs to be faced firmly in guiding the computer culture.

We must make sure that the possession of a computer never becomes a "status symbol," something that is there in order to keep up with the Joneses. We should think of ourselves as lucky to have computers but should be acutely aware that it is just plain wrong that other children do not. We should think of ourselves as campaigners for more universal access to computers.

Beyond taking a verbal stance it is important that we do what we can to make available to others the privilege we have. For example, you can take advantage of your computer to acquire skills that will enable you to volunteer as a computer instructor at a local science museum, community center or school, where expertise might be in short supply.

Perhaps more important is how you discuss in your family the development of cyberculture as reflected in the writings of cyber-topians, the magazines of the "wired lifestyle" and in movies and on television. There are powerful moral themes in this larger cyberculture. Some are good. Others are dangerous.

The culture of the Internet has a strong egalitarian streak: The mature billionaire and the ten-year-old kid are supposed to have the same privileges of access to virtual places on the Net. There is a strong defense of free speech on the Internet. There is also a strong pro-environmental movement.

But on the negative side, there is a tendency to value technical achievement for its own sake. **Bill Gates** writes about the wonders of this world in highly materialistic terms. For example, his house will be so computerized and so "intelligent" that it will know when to turn on the lights and what music to play in each room by keeping track of where you are and inferring your likes and dislikes from your past behavior.

Would you like such a house? I must admit that I am enough of a "technology freak" to want to see and even own such things. On the other hand, I do not count them as important and am quite nervous about a generation growing up with such things at the center of their sense of achievement.

# Intellectual Property

One of the more interesting and unexpected phenomena I have noticed while observing children using computers in schools is the concept of ownership of entities that are less material than toys or houses or money.

A LEARNING STORY

# Owning Ideas

In a school in which fourth-grade children learned to program in **Logo**, Mary discovered how to make colors on the screen flash with an attractive scintillation. The arrangement of the computers and the culture of the class encouraged students to look at one another's work, and Mary's soon drew numerous oohs and ahs. When students asked, "How did you get it to do that?" she was delighted, and happily explained her idea.

The next day her feelings changed when she observed similar effects on many screens. Fighting back tears, she complained to a teacher that everyone was stealing her idea—and some had even incorporated pieces of her program in their own.

The teacher comforted her and said, "But aren't you proud to see people using your procedures?"

"Well, yes," Mary said with hesitation in her voice, but the idea was planted in her mind. When class members came together later she raised the issue for discussion. Solutions for her concern were explored, including the idea that it was good to take procedures from others, but that credit should be given and something like a patent office established where ideas could be registered.

---

Of course similar situations arise in schools and families without computers. An idea for a story or a style of drawing can be taken over in ways that elicit accusations of plagiarism. But the issue of ownership of an intellectual property is seldom as direct as in Mary's case, in which something more developed and specific than an abstract idea was taken over. It is in the nature of programming that ideas are embodied as "code" that can be directly copied and used as a component of a different construct by another programmer. Moreover, this is not an occasional situation; it is central to the spirit of programming.

So students like Mary are drawn into serious, personally motivated discussion about ways in which taking an idea from someone is like, and ways in which it is unlike, taking a material thing. How this is resolved depends on the **culture of the classroom** (or home) in which it takes place. I have observed many discussions in which respect for intellectual property developed and a growing sense emerged that nonmaterial possessions could be more valuable than physical things, and all the more so to the extent that they are disseminated and used by other people.

# Dangers on the Net

The most positive side of the Internet's culture from a humanitarian perspective is its potential for leveling. Its dominant ideology has it that everyone has access to the same resources. This may not be strictly true, but it is surely more true than in most sectors of our society.

But the very features that make for leveling also hold the potential for **deception** and seduction. Your child can now knock on the digital door of knowledge sources that were previously open only to small numbers of researchers. A child can talk with an expert in a shared area of interest. The advantages are immense. But by the same token the risks are serious. People you might consider to be unsuitable company can now knock on your *children's* digital door, gaining access to the home through the computer. And if children can gain access to NASA's collection of space pictures, in principle they can gain access to someone's collection of pornography.

In practice, the current danger in this extreme form has been greatly exaggerated in the media. Pornography on the Internet is not easy to find, and the number of reported cases of seduction is minute compared with those that happen in other contexts. But the danger cannot be written off, as even a small number is unacceptable and the situation could grow worse. And besides, the more serious danger may lie not in these extreme pathological forms but in what many quite "normal" people who use the Net see as innocent social behavior.

The most talked-about example of this social behavior is **deception on the Internet**, where an entire culture of false personalities has grown with amazing rapidity. Is it a breach of morality if the dog in the now-famous cartoon allows his email correspondents to think he isn't a dog? Or is this in the same class as the acceptable old tradition of masked balls? Is it dangerous if teenagers would like to get into conversations with older people who would not take them seriously if they knew their ages?

There are two kinds of protection parents can use against such dangers.

The first is to try to block their children from making undesirable contacts. This can be done in many ways. There is much talk of using a combination of rating systems and special software or chips that will allow a parent to block a computer from communicating with sites that have bad ratings. Another variant is to allow children to communicate with just one site, which will act as a more effectively controlled gateway to the wider Net than could be achieved using a chip.

I am sure that most parents will adopt some such measures. But a more fundamental approach is needed: the protection that comes from a **family culture** of trust and truthfulness. Without that, all the technical methods that will ever be invented will have leaks: Ingenious children, or ingenious psycho-marauders, will find a way through.

**Honesty** does not exclude participating in Internet activities based on assumed identities. As a form of drama, such activities can be psychologically healthy and ethically honest provided that the participants understand them as a kind of play. You cannot control how others understand their participation. What you can do is establish an understanding in your family that whatever is not open is suspect, and that "weird" behaviors are something to be shared and discussed rather than something taboo to be peeped at and not mentioned for fear of reprimand or snigger.

Parents are worried about ways in which their children can be deceived. They are right. But once more, consistency is a precondition for moral standards. A family that wants to fight deception must create a culture of absolute honesty. If you can't (for whatever reason) or do not want to do this everywhere, at the very least it should be done by insisting on (and practicing!) the highest standards of honesty in the home computer culture. Children who realize that in some areas of life the line between truth and falsity is necessarily hazy can still understand that in one area it is clear-cut.

# Family

## Family Computer Learning Culture

In October 1995 *Time* Magazine was experimenting with the idea of launching "Time Digital" to deal with events in the rapidly expanding world of digital things. The editors commissioned three articles on what they thought were the most common concerns about computers: their effect on work, their effect on language and their effect on children. I was asked to write the children article and expressed a family-oriented position rather like what I am saying here.

My bottom line was that parents should recognize the need to build new kinds of relationships with their children and should see the computer as a vehicle for building, rather than as an obstacle to, family cohesion. Parents should spend less time worrying about what the kids are doing or are not doing with computers and more time trying to find common interests or projects to do together. The article suggested using the children's enthusiasm for computers as a basis for enhancing the family's **learning culture**.

The word **culture** is used in lots of different ways. Some meanings are a little snobbish: People often refer to others as "cultured" if they read certain kinds of books and like certain kinds of music. I am using it here in a more homey sense, more like what people mean when they say they want their children to understand the culture of the country that their immigrant grandparents came from. In this sense culture refers to such things as the ways of thinking, the traditions, the beliefs, the kinds of jokes and the values that are shared by all people in a country. I use phrases like the **family learning culture** in a similar sense to refer to a family's way of thinking about learning—its beliefs, preferred activities and traditions associated with learning.

The idea of a culture implies some coherence and agreement. It does not mean that everyone in the family agrees about everything. In fact, what might make one family learning culture different from another is how each deals with differences in **learning styles**. One family might tolerate just one way to learn, while another might recognize and even celebrate differences. In a healthy family culture there will be both a basis of agreement and an understanding of differences.

A basic question about a family's learning culture is whether it values learning. I assume that you would not be reading this book if you did not attach importance to some kinds of learning. But what kinds? Some families don't care about learning in itself but value some of its outer signs, such as school grades, which may be important for practical reasons later. Some value learning the skills of a particular hobby or sport. In one family, people take delight in recounting a learning experience in the office, the playing field or the kitchen. In another, talk of learning is confined to comments on school report cards.

Thinking about issues like these is a step towards correcting the weakness of a learning culture in which nobody ever talks about learning. Talking about learning may be the best way to improve it.

The relationship between the computer and the family learning culture is a two-way street: The computer will affect the learning culture and the learning culture will affect what you do with the computer. The computer is a touchstone of differences in attitudes about learning. I have mentioned how watching children at work with computers can lead parents to have more respect for what their children are capable of learning. It can reveal prejudices about what is appropriate at different ages. Dad's reaction could be delight or irritation when a ten-year-old learns to use the newly arrived computer faster and better. When children believe that parents can't learn about computers (or the VCR), that says something about the family learning culture. Or if people are surprised when a grandmother of eighty or a grandson of two succeeds in using a computer, that too says a great deal about their learning culture.

Computer learning experiences give the family a chance to become more aware of its learning culture and a chance to work at slowly (cultures never change fast) improving it. And, as the learning culture in the family becomes clearer and more self-conscious, it will influence the kinds of computer experiences that family members engage in. New understanding of learning in general might draw you as well as your children into activities with the computer whose value you might not previously have recognized. It might also make you more confident in your own willingness to learn new things including, but not only, some related to computers.

Developing your home computer learning culture includes something of what intelligent families have always done in relation to children and other media such as movies and books. Good parenting in the area of movies includes seeing some movies together (and some not), appreciating them together, talking about them and criticizing them together. It does not include the thinking of a mother who told me, "The kids are watching mindless TV, a perfect activity for a summer Saturday morning." Relaxation and fun are good things but neither imply mindlessness.

In my own extended family, where children are grown up and grandchildren are giving us a second chance, it means a constant search for movies that can be genuinely shared by adults and grandchildren of all ages. For example, last summer, when the grandchildren could spend more time with us than during the school year, we all had a great time with *Charlotte's Web*, *Dumbo*, *Twenty Thousand Leagues Under the Sea*, *Horton* and several science videos. References to these have become part of the family culture. My own participation included looking for movies, watching them and talking about them. It also included bending my own summer reading a little, for example by spending some enjoyable hours with E.B. White's essays to see what I could learn about how he came to write the book *Charlotte's Web*, and by rereading the book to compare it more closely with the movie.

High-quality shareable classics in the digital field are just beginning to emerge, and you should be looking out for productions that can be enjoyed by adults with developed taste as well as by children who are getting there. In my own family, the game *Myst* proved to be a good example for the older grandchildren and their parents. An eight-year-old can get into it and an adult still enjoy it. I had a good time with a six-year-old and a CD-ROM version of *Peter and the Wolf.* This year, because the children are older and because more material is accessible than it was last year, I expect activities on the World Wide Web to have a bigger role and have begun to browse in search of shareable Web activities. One of these will be discussed in Chapter 6.

I use movies and books as examples to make certain points about the **computer culture** because they are familiar, but in the very near future the separation of "books," "movies" and "computers" will seem quaint and old-fashioned.

Technologically speaking, the merger of movies and computers will take place as more computer power is placed in "home entertainment centers" and better images appear on computer screens. I don't know whether people will say that the TV now serves as a computer or that the computer now serves as the TV. A more important form of merger for the family learning culture will be using the hybrid computer/VCR/TV—whatever you call it—to make home movies that will break out of what I called the theater + camera stage. The ability to store and edit and combine digital versions of high-quality moving images will open a whole new area of activity, with unprecedented potential for intellectually and artistically rich projects of family collaboration.

Reading and writing have become so much the symbol for what is most important in children's learning that any suggestion of merging books with movies and computers evokes extremely strong feelings. But it will happen. The first step will be a little device (it will be a computer, though the manufacturers will avoid calling it that) about the size of a small book, much lighter and fitted with a screen with enough resolution for a quality of type and graphics superior to what we find in typical contemporary books. It will have enough memory to store many books at a time.

What reason could there be to prefer reading print on paper? Yes, you will be able to "flip the pages," and if people really like it to have the feel/texture of a leather binding or even to emanate the smell of leather, I am sure that enterprising manufacturers will oblige.

And once such a thing becomes common, what reason will there be for illustrators to confine themselves to still drawings? Why not movies?

These predictions raise many large issues. Here I want to emphasize just one: A home learning culture that excludes computers or insists too hard on the separation from other media will be placed under increasing stress as the boundaries between media shift and fade. If you want yours to avoid instability and tension you will do better to anticipate the trends than wait for them to impose themselves.

■

# Advice to Parents: Learn Something

A lot, or even most, learning done by young children is more like taking in the culture of the family than being taught individual facts or skills by you or by a computer program. Acquiring language is a clear example of something virtually everyone learns mostly without direct, deliberate teaching.

Number and logic puzzles are examples of content that a learning culture can include or leave out. If you happen to like puzzles, they provide a good way to learn problem-solving skills. But there are plenty of other good ways. The one aspect of a good learning culture that is *not* optional is being rich in good examples of enthusiastic learning. *I see it as extremely important for children to see adults engaged in learning.* It is important for them to share learning experiences with adults but also to see that adults value learning for themselves and not only for the kids.

One obvious way your computer can contribute to developing the **home learning culture** is by constantly challenging you to learn to use it. There is an endless supply of new computer skills to acquire. You should learn some of these with your children. Indeed some of them can probably be learned *from* your children. But you should also be ready to talk in an uninhibited way with your children about learning you did on your own and about the difficulties you encountered, whether you overcame them or not.

Another way is using the computer as a medium for learning something of value to you that is not in itself related to computers. Doing a little more learning yourself might bring you real pleasures, as well as contribute to strengthening the family learning culture for the children. It can also give you a deeper sense of how software can (and how it cannot) contribute to learning. *Unless you have used a computer to learn something yourself, you are not in a good position to think about how it can help children learn.*

My own quest for good examples of software that would help me learn has been a little disappointing. I have not found many. But among those I can recommend, I would single out a style of music program developed by the musicologist Robert Winter and the pioneering multimedia publishing company Voyager. CD-ROM productions in this style are presentations of musical works based on the fact that CD-ROMs are musical CDs but also much more. You can use them to listen to the music. If you wish, you can also see on the computer screen a running commentary on the music as you hear it. You can also stop at any point and go back to an earlier point. You can see on the screen an overview of the whole piece and play any major section instantaneously.

To my taste this is an excellent use of digital media for learning. It does not try to ram anything down my throat, but allows me new freedom in exploring something that interests me. I have found not only that it allows me a better relationship with individual musical works but a deeper understanding of music.

# Treat Parents Gently

It will mostly be parents who buy this book. But I hope that kids who are old enough will read it too, and that older siblings or parents will bring some of its ideas to those who are not yet able to read it for themselves.

One thing I've been saying over and over again is that parents should learn from their kids. Of course kids should also learn from parents. I say this less often because everyone knows that. But the point is that it goes both ways.

This is especially true when it comes to computers. Some parents know very little about computers and are nervous about trying. If you want to help them you must understand their feelings and treat them gently. Hold their hands. Hug them—but don't do it in a condescending way.

Other parents know a lot about computers but just don't get it about how kids work with them. You have to help them. But remember that people have different **styles of working** and of learning. Different strokes for different folks.

When I talk about how kids work with computers, I do not mean to insult you by suggesting that you have a kind of "childish" way of doing things. If you get to know me better by reading this book and looking at the CD-ROM, you will understand that I personally prefer—and usually use—the style I see most kids using. And I am not the only one; many of the most brilliant programmers work in this way. But many adults like to do it in another way. And some of these are also very brilliant people.

Actually there are lots of differences in styles of work—just as there are lots of differences in styles of clothing or music. Right now I want to talk about one big difference.

The other day someone told me: "The secret of using computers is to know that you have to do everything *exactly* the way the computer expects." Well, this is right in one sense. But it is wrong in a more profound sense. If you do the "wrong" thing the sky doesn't fall down on you. You don't get shot. The computer doesn't break. The fact is that many people learn about computers by poking around, doing this or that and eventually getting it. And *then* you do the "right thing." Sometimes people call this process "trial and error"; I prefer the French word: **bricolage**. If you really hate using foreign words you could translate it without too much loss of meaning as "tinkerer."

The person who told me his "secret" does things differently; he has a different learning style. He hates touching a key until he is sure he knows what will happen—maybe from reading the manual or from asking someone who has already been there. Since people like my friend feel lost without a precise plan, I shall refer to them as Planners, using a capital P to indicate that these are people who attach very special importance to Plans. Of course they are not the only people who make plans. We all do; we are all planners (without a capital p). But Planners like to have much more precise plans than **Bricoleurs** and are more reluctant to change their plans.

Planners often do very well with computers, but my friend was quite wrong in thinking that his style was the only one that would work. Bricolage works as well in most situations. For me it usually works better, but that's because of the way I think, not because one style is better for everyone.

One should never generalize about such things, but I do have some observations about who is likely to be a Planner and who is likely to be a Bricoleur. If you could count what fraction of kids are Planners and what fraction of adults, I am sure you would find that the adult fraction is much bigger: Adults are more likely than kids to be Planners. If you did the same count for women compared with men, I believe you would find that men are more likely than women to be Planners.

So if you are a Bricoleur and you want to work with your dad, you should be aware that there is a good chance he will be a Planner, and if you don't make allowance for this there will surely be more misunderstandings between you than are really necessary. But then it might turn out that you are the Planner and your Dad is the Bricoleur. Generalizations are never strictly true. The important thing is to know that these differences exist and to make allowance for them. Don't get mad if someone doesn't do things the same way as you. But also don't feel put down if it is someone you respect—your way might be just as good.

# Computer as Bore

The image of a love affair between children and computers suggests that all children are caught up in it. But many children are simply not interested in computers and some actually dislike them.

Some parents worry: If my kids don't like computers does this mean there is something wrong with them? And what should I do about it?

It certainly does not mean there is something wrong with the *kids*. But perhaps it means that *there is something very wrong with the learning environment of the home or of the school.* I do not mean to say that there are no excellent learning environments without computers. Quite the contrary. I am only saying that if a kid living in a typical home going to a typical school does not like computers, this is very often a sign of something wrong.

Adults who don't like computers will object: Why does it mean that there is something wrong? Everyone has different tastes. Some like spinach and some hate it. Some like jazz and some like Bach. There isn't anything everyone likes.

Sounds plausible, but look more closely. Some like jazz and some like classical music and some like rock and roll and some people in distant lands like kinds of music that Americans might not even recognize as music. But not liking any kind of music at all is so rare that it is grounds for suspecting that something is wrong.

The question we have to ask is whether to put *not liking computers* with not liking Bach or with *not liking music.* Many people would put it with not liking a particular kind of music. In my experience, a closer look always reveals that these people have had a very limited experience of what can be done with computers. As if they had heard only one kind of music—which was badly performed into the bargain—and decided that music was not for them.

Of course it can happen that someone simply does not care for any kind of music. More commonly it can very well happen that someone who was positively engaged with music in the past, and will again be in the future, happens right now to be so deeply in something else that even music simply seems irrelevant. And what is true of music can be true of computers as well.

So if you are a person who is "not interested in computers," please understand that I am not trying to thrust them on you or to persuade parents or others in a position of power to thrust them on you. What I am saying is that very often people get to have negative attitudes because they have seen the computer only in a narrow way. This may be your case. And if it is you may find that computers in some different guise or different use are more to your liking.

Lets look at two simple examples of how kids can be turned off computers.

I have seen a first-grade class introduced to computers this way: The children sit in pairs in front of the computer for instruction in something called "keyboarding." One child works the keys and the other the mouse.

B. . . O. . . R. . . I. . . N. . . G

Or think about this one. In the classroom there are far fewer computers than students. Access is not regulated. So naturally a climate of aggression develops. The pushier students get at the machines. Some of the less pushy give up and decide that computers are not for them. Very often this is a girl deciding that computers are for boys, and a gender stereotype grows.

An intellectually active kid who associates the computer with boring activities or a gentle kid who associates it with aggression are two causes of turn-off that can and should be removed. I am sure you do not have to be told that there can also be more subtle reasons for acquiring a distaste.

To parents I would say: Before you make up your mind why a child in your family does not like computers, take a careful look at the whole situation. Discuss it with your child. Find out about experiences that might have led to negative attitudes. But in the end be sensitive to the wonderful complexity of individual tastes. And most important, remember that the true gift of the computer and the true core of the love affair is enhancing individual choice and independence. To force the computer on a reluctant child would contradict the most valuable advantage of having a positive relationship with the computer.

The presence of the computer has to be seen as part of the psychologically complex web of relationships and feelings that make up a family. Some children might reject the computer because they perceive it as being forced on them and are at a stage when they are asserting independence. Rejection of the computer might really be rejection of a parent. Factors such as these call for careful attention to the dynamics of the family and are not easily remedied. Yet the main step I recommend for the easy case may, if it is carried out sensitively, contribute to healing grave family disorders:

Just take seriously the analogy with tastes in music. As I believe that everybody will like some kind of music in some kind of context, I believe too that the computer can be used in so many ways for so many different purposes that *in principle* every person will find some way of using computers both useful and congenial.

The qualification "in principle" is significant. The ways in which the computer might be congenial and useful for some people might not yet have been developed. More likely such ways have been developed but are not easily found. Fortunately the rapid growth of the world of computers increases almost week by week not only the range of programs available but also the availability of help in searching for them.

# Advice for Girls and Boys

Parents often ask me about differences between boys and girls. A parent who has bought a computer for a son and wants to know whether to buy a computer for a daughter gets my simple and blunt answer: Sex has nothing to do with it.

But here's a different situation. Kathy has two brothers and a father who do a lot with the computer. When she is at the computer, whether with the others or by herself, she feels uneasy and suspects that this is because it's a "boy's thing." *She is probably right.* But I am not contradicting myself. The three males in this family have made the computer into a "male thing." This may be partly because of how the computer is set up, including what kind of software it has, but it is more likely to be because of something about the **family culture**. The "male thing" is not about the physical computer that came in a box; it is about what Sherry Turkle has called the "subjective computer"–the idea of the computer constructed in people's heads.

My advice to children in the first of these families is to stick up for being the same. My advice to Kathy is to stick up for being different. If the family can afford it they should get a second computer. In the long run she, and everyone who will listen, should be trying to understand what's going on in this family's culture. How sexist is it? How sexist does it want to be?

I respond in the same spirit to questions about studies showing there are differences in **styles of usage**. Yes, there probably are–statistically speaking. But you aren't a statistic. You are a person, and should stand up for your right to be what you are and deal with the others in your family as what they are.

# Advice for Grandparents

Most grandparents I know complain about not having enough time with their grandchildren. If you are one of these, here's your chance. But if you happen to be one of those who have more time with grandchildren than you know what to do with, well, this may still be your chance. I'm going to talk here about ways that the computer can solve both these problems and be a source of great joy even for those who suffer from neither.

Of course, what the computer can offer you depends on how much effort you are ready to make. I'll start from the minimal end and build up to more demanding but also more rewarding things to do.

## Giving Gifts

A grandparent who does not know a thing about computers, and does not want to, may still be able to score a hit by giving computer-related gifts. You don't need me to tell you that anyone, kids included, who gets into the computer world quickly develops an insatiable appetite for computer stuff, and browsing through Chapter 6 and the Resource Guide may give you some ideas about how to choose.

## Giving Attention

One step up from this minimal commitment is to take an intelligent interest in what your grandchildren do with the computer. Sit down with them—don't be afraid to get near the machine, the kid will protect you—and let them show you something they made or something they can do. If they don't have anything to show you except games that you can't follow, or math or reading programs that you find totally boring, your grandchildren are probably being deprived of the best kinds of computer activity. And in this case you have a golden opportunity to do something really good for them. Go to it!

They should at least be able to show you art work they have made or animations or desk-top publishing. If they prefer science to art they might be able to show you a report or study of some kind or a simulation. Or they might be able to take you on a tour through the Web. Or demonstrate a CD-ROM. Or show you how email works. If they don't know about these things or don't have the software or hardware to do them, you have a great opportunity to do something *for* them that might turn into something to do *with* them.

## Providing a Pupil

On the other hand, if they do show you something interesting, you get a chance to have them show you how they do it. If you pay attention you'll begin to learn what can be done with computers. You will be getting something. But this is a case where receiving is giving, for having you as a pupil can be a rewarding experience for the kids. Make the most of it. Do some homework when you are not with them to enhance the experience of being together.

If you think this is too difficult, read the story of how my eighty-plus-year-old mother learned to use a computer. Check out the interactive lesson on the CD-ROM at the back of this book.

## Being in Touch

If you have your own computer you can use it to be in closer touch with the grandchildren. Try it. You will see that it allows richer kinds of communication that go beyond what you can do with the phone.

The popular image of communicating by computer is sending email, and many people might think of this as too reduced and impersonal a channel for communicating with their grandchildren—even if the children are old enough to write. So it is. But the possibilities of electronic communication are rapidly expanding as software becomes available to send drawings—even animated drawings—and even to see one another's image on the screen so that you can have a weekly or even daily teleconference.

## Sharing Projects

Here are examples of projects you can do with your grandchildren that will be all the more interesting the more the family is scattered across the country.

Share a digital photo album of all the family members' latest activities. When you get your next roll of photos developed, ask to have them on computer disk. (My local drugstore in rural Maine offers this service for just a few dollars!) If you can't do it yourself, putting these on the computer is a great project for your grandchildren. The younger ones may simply post them up on decorated backgrounds while the older ones will use them to create a multimedia show. Take this idea a step further by building up a family history on the computer. The kids can contribute the computer skills while you contribute knowledge of what happened to Great Uncle Nathaniel way back then.

Design a family trip on the Internet. Tell your grandchild that what you would like for your birthday is a trip in cyberspace. For weeks beforehand the young tour guide can be busy checking out sites that might interest you.

## Getting Hooked

I'll take a bet with you that after a few months of getting involved with computer activities because you think they are good for your grandchildren you will begin doing some just for yourself . . .

## Adopt A Grandkid

If you don't have any grandchildren or not enough to keep you busy you might think about becoming a surrogate grandparent. There are many children in the world whose lives could be enriched by developing a relationship with you. Even before there were computers many retired people did good for the world and for their own sense of relevance by volunteering to work with children in schools, museums, parks and hospitals. The computer presence opens vast new horizons for this kind of service. Even people who cannot move out of their bedrooms can use electronic communications to establish enriching relationships with children.

Both of the following stories have something to say to grandparents. The first is about your own learning and the second about what you can do for your grandchildren. But really they are both about both subjects.

# A Kid Aged Eighty

When she was eighty my mother said: "You know, I'm sorry I didn't take up your offer to teach me about computers when I was seventy. Now I'd really like to know but it's far too late."

I knew better than to argue but went out and bought her a computer, one of the first generation of Macs.

Mother had a particular goal in mind. World events had taken her and her friends far from their country of origin. She liked to stay in touch with friends scattered across three continents by letter. However her finger joints were developing arthritis, and holding a pen was becoming increasingly uncomfortable. She correctly perceived that the computer would be the right instrument for her. The keys would respond to a light touch. She would not have to do the mechanical adjustments needed for a typewriter. But the idea seemed simply out of range. "The computer was for young people." She was eighty. And many years had passed since the last time she remembered learning something really new.

But it wasn't very difficult after all to learn enough to get started. . . just enough to write a letter without even worrying much about correcting mistakes and certainly not at all about format. So her first letter went out and she was thrilled.

I see in this a simple but important lesson about learning. Get going! Choose a realistic goal and do it. Don't worry about the imaginary inspector looking over your shoulder.

But the events of the next months brought another lesson. Mother learned a lot more and I believe better than she would have ten years earlier, when she would have been more jealous of her time and more impatient to get results. I saw the way she learned as rather like the way she would take her walk in the public gardens across the road from where she lived. Every day she would go out without any more goal than walking though a terrain she knew and loved. On some days something special might happen; perhaps she would see a particularly beautiful flower or observe an incident. She wasn't looking for these things but when they happened they were enjoyed, often remembered and sometimes recounted. If nothing interesting happened on any particular day, no big deal.

There was something similar in the way she related to her computer. She learned by browsing, like people who surf the Internet and like most kids who pick up the enormous knowledge they acquire about computers. Mother would pass the time simply playing with her computer, trying this or that. There was no goal like those set in school lessons: Today I will learn something specific. But when she found something interesting or new or useful she would be pleased and would often remember it and sometimes use it in her letter writing. So little by little she became more proficient and began to do more sophisticated operations, such as writing her letter in a big font she could read more easily and then putting it into a smaller font to print it. Most important, she became comfortable with the machine.

I tell this story as if it were about an old lady learning the simplest computer skills. In fact it is about much more. It is about the way I have learned most of what I know about computers. I think it is about the kind of learning used by most of the virtuoso people whose knowledge of the details of computer functioning exceeds mine by as much as mine exceeded my mother's. Of course there are people who learn about computers in the school-style way of following a curriculum. There are different styles of learning. But the school-style one has had more than its share of attention . . . I think the other style needs to get equal time. Especially important here is the fact that the exploratory style is preferred by most children, and I want to assure parents that they do not have to force the curriculum style on their children. Many parents and teachers are blind to the exploratory style and observe children engaged in it as wasting their time.

# Grandson Sam

Sam was barely learning to talk when it became apparent that geometric shapes had a very special interest for him. So I did something that might sound like something only a specialist could do, but in fact most parents—or grandparents—with a little self-confidence could learn to do it in less time than they spend on dealing with a child's minor ailments or clothing.

I made a computer program matched to Sam's interests.

It did not do very much. Hitting different keys would make shapes appear on the screen. Other keys would make them take on different colors. If this were happening today instead of six years ago, I would take advantage of greater speed in the machines and more powerful programming software that has come in its wake to make the shapes move and interact. But perhaps the desire to do this reflects the prevalent taste for fancy graphics and snappy animation. In fact Sam's **game** was very sparse in its aesthetic. The computer magazine reviewers would no doubt have shrugged it off as a piece of nothing. But Sam loved it.

So what?

So: Making this program was part of developing my relationship with Sam. It gave him a lot of opportunity to use his growing vocabulary for shapes. Everyone in the family was taken by the charming way he would say something like "par-lell-lel-lel-la-la-gam" before he had enough pronunciation control to get the word right. He was appreciating the keyboard in a purposive way and did not have to go through the stage many children experience of hitting meaninglessly at keys in imitation of what they see their computer-using parents do. And who knows what else.

We believe that Sam appropriated the idea that a string of letters could have a personal use when he wanted to save drawings made using KidPix (a best-selling program used by children to "paint" on the computer screen). To save drawings one has (at least for the moment; I'm sure this will soon change) to spell out on the keyboard a name so that it can be filed away in the computer memory and later retrieved. The first few times, Sam would call an adult to do this. But he wanted independence and eventually got it by learning to type the names himself. Soon after that he began to read.

Sam's interests moved from what seemed to be very "cerebral" directions into painting when I gave him KidPix. He quickly developed an enthusiasm for computer painting. He must have done a thousand of them before one day deciding to move to paper, pencil, crayons and paints as richer media and thereafter only very occasionally used the computer as a drawing medium.

## A Cautionary Note: At What Age Should Children Use Computers?

This is a badly formed question, like asking: At what age should children use crayons or dolls? There can be no answer because a computer is not a thing with one use.

And in the near future it will be less and less a thing with one form. Soon an infant's computer might look like the stuffed objects that nobody minds giving to babies almost from birth. The baby will use it by hitting it, touching it, gurgling or yelling at it, watching what it does and hearing the sounds it makes.

Computers can be used well at all ages. They can also be abused at all ages.

I am fearful of using computers as "baby stimulators" and "baby-sitters" by exploiting their holding power before we understand it enough to use it wisely.

I am fearful of the idea that children can be better prepared for life by doing schoolish kinds of learning at the earliest possible age. This idea has been severely criticized by many psychologists, perhaps most eloquently by **David Elkind** in his book *The Hurried Child*. To these old objections I add a new one: The computer opens opportunities for new forms of learning that are far more consistent with the nature of the young child. How absurd then to use it to impose old forms.

■

# A Lad and a Lady

Near where I live in rural Maine, a lady of eighty, whom I shall call Lydia T...., has transformed her life by joining the thirty (or so) million users of the Internet. At a stage in her life and at a time of social movement away from the extended family, when many like her would be living in disconnected isolation, Lydia T.... is in contact with more people than she had ever imagined possible. Among them is a boy of eight with whom she has developed an especially strong relationship. His life too has been transformed. Although Lydia T.... has never seen him, she has time to spend with him in electronic contact, to guide him and to help him emotionally and intellectually over hurdles in his school life.

Lydia and the boy are in great need of one another because social changes that came in the wake of technology have undermined the cohesive extended family. There is something poetic and hopeful in the possibility that newer technologies can at least partially undo the resulting isolation. It seems to me quite obvious that this could happen on a scale large enough to have significant consequences for the rehabilitation of the learning environment. Imagine the consequences of having several hundred thousand Lydias in touch with several million kids!

# Extended Family

The story has many powerful morals for thinking about computers and learning. One of them is that you, whoever you are, can enrich the meaning of the computer presence in your life and your family's by making a contribution to something larger. Even if nobody in your family is actually eight or eighty, with a little imagination you will easily think of something you can do in the same spirit. Indeed, drawing your children into the conception as well as the implementation of such a project might well become one of the best uses of the computer presence you will ever make.

A different kind of moral of the Lydia T.... story is that good learning can be mediated by computers without any of the kinds of software that are labeled "educational" or "edutainment." This is one of many situations that set me ruminating about how often what we call education (whether we are talking about software or not) is a poor substitute for real life and real relationships. What Lydia is giving and getting uses only the technologically simplest form of what the Net has to offer. Yet this email alone is sufficient to be a breakthrough in establishing communication between people who have something to say to one another and benefit from it.

Of course technology alone is not going to do it on a socially significant scale. What an eighty-year-old lady and an eight-year-old boy will find to say to one another depends on who they are and how well the match-making was organized (or allowed to self-organize) and on how they were introduced. Most attempts to set up pen-pal relationships through email degenerate into the exchange of platitudes. But it is easy to see that it could work if the child has a real need for a confidante or a guide or perhaps even simply for help on a personal project or school work.

I know critics who respond to the story of Lydia T.... with a knee-jerk: "Lovely story, but you didn't need a computer."

Well, yes and no. I can tell you many moving stories about older and younger people being brought together with nary a computer in sight. The question is whether what happened could not be enormously extended with more connected computers.

Consider for example the work of Kathleen Lefevre, one of the most gifted special education teachers I have known. For many years she took her class of troubled children at a New York City public school to visit and work with people in a retirement home. She has successfully encouraged the development of relationships in which the older people talk about how things were long ago, and older and younger work together to get something down on paper, often in the form of a poem.

Kathleen Lefevre did wonderful things for the young and for the old participants in her project. Where such personal contact can be arranged and where it works it is obvious that no sensible person would suggest replacing it by computer contact. But it is equally obvious that the budding relationship could be strengthened if one or the other of the participants could contribute something to it at any time of the day or night. And in addition I can't help thinking that with this extra channel of being in touch, the relationships would have had a better chance of surviving when the school board decided to chop the budget and eliminate all such programs.

Another story also comes from experience in a school context that could be extended, enriched and made more stable by being placed in the context of a computer-connected community on a wider scale.

This one is about work by my students and a group of teachers in an innercity Boston public school, where students have access for about an hour a day to networked computers donated by **IBM**. This is where Idit Harel, working with Teresa M., carried out the precursor to the story of the anatomy of the slug. The essential innovation was to give the students the opportunity to work for most of a school year on a single project aimed at making their version of a kind of commercial software. When Idit graduated with a Ph.D. from M.I.T. for this work and went on to do bigger things in the world, the baton was taken over by Yasmin Kafai, who switched the content of the projects from making educational software to making an educational **game**. Both Idit and Yasmin have written books about their experiences which give deep insights into the learning that can take place in doing such work. The next phase, which is now nearing completion, is being conducted by Michele Evard, also as a doctoral project.

Michele's innovation is what brings us back to the discussion started by the story of Lydia T..... She has set up a system that allows the students who worked on the project the previous year to participate as consultants to the newcomers. It works like this: Anyone who has a problem can send a message into the computer system. Anyone who wants to participate as a consultant can read the requests for help and send back advice. As you might expect, Michele is finding that some students are more eager than others to enter the consultant role. She does not mind that: In the laboratory we are all committed to the idea that students be allowed to choose their learning paths. But a substantial number do participate, and it is very clear that the benefits accrue to both sides. Giving advice involves as much learning as taking it.

I remember the loneliness I often felt in my school days when I developed interests that were not shared by anyone I knew. Yet surely some like-minded person somewhere in the world, perhaps just up the road, had interests close enough to mine for us to have had the most marvelously rich experiences together. Yet there was no way short of sheer chance (which did happen once or twice in my life) of finding that person. I don't say that this situation of eager minds trapped in isolation from one another has completely changed. But we do have the instruments to change it. The social structure to use the instrument will come. Especially if you help it happen and help yourself in so doing.

# Helping

The advice in much of this book comes directly from my own experience. But in these days of the Internet we should not have to rely so much on ourselves. So I checked to see what the Internet could give me by way of advice about how to treat fellow family members who might be having computer troubles. Here I give you this sample as an teaser. It was downloaded from an "ezine"—an electronic magazine you can read yourself through your computer. The following piece is by Phil Agre, reprinted here with his permission.

*Computer people are generally fine human beings, but nonetheless they do a lot of inadvertent harm in the ways that they "help" other people with their computer problems. Now that we're trying to get everyone on the net, I thought it might be helpful to write down in one place everything I've been taught about how to help people use computers.*

*First you have to tell yourself some things:*

■ *Nobody is born knowing this stuff.*

■ *You've forgotten what it's like to be a beginner.*

■ *If it's not obvious to them, it's not obvious.*

■ *A computer is a means to an end. The person you're helping probably cares mostly about the end. This is reasonable.*

■ *They probably don't need to know how it works. You'd probably be embarrassed to tell them how it really works anyway.*

■ *The best way to learn is through apprenticeship—that is, by doing some real task together with someone who has skills that you don't have.*

■ *Your goal is not to solve their problem. Your goal is to help them become one notch more capable of solving their problem on their own.*

103

■ *Most user interfaces are terrible. When people make mistakes it's usually the fault of the interface. You've forgotten how many ways you've learned to adapt to bad interfaces. You've forgotten how many things you once assumed that the interface would be able to do for you.*

■ *Knowledge lives in communities, not individuals. A computer user who's not part of a community of computer users is going to have a harder time of it than one who is.*

■ *By the time they ask you for help, they've probably tried several different things. As a result, their computer might be in a strange state. That's not their fault.*

*Having convinced yourself of these things, you will find yourself much more willing to do these things:*

■ *Never do something for someone that they are capable of doing for themselves.*

■ *Don't take the keyboard. Let them do all the typing, even if it's slower that way, and even if you have to point them to each and every key they need to type. That's the only way they're going to learn from the interaction.*

■ *Be aware of how abstract your language is. For example, "Get into the editor" is abstract and "press this key" is concrete. Don't say anything unless you intend for them to understand it. Keep adjusting your language downward towards concrete units until they start to get it, then slowly adjust back up towards greater abstraction so long as they're following you. When formulating a take-home lesson ("when it does this and that, you should check such-and-such"), check once again that you're using language of the right degree of abstraction for this user right now.*

■ *Attend to the symbolism of the interaction. In particular, try not to tower over them. If at all possible, squat down so your eyes are just below the level of theirs. When they're looking at the com-*

*puter, look at the computer. When they're looking at you, look
back at them.*

■ *If something is true, explain how they can see it's true.*

■ *Find out what they're really trying to do. Is there another way to
go about it?*

■ *Whenever they start to blame themselves, blame the computer, no
matter how many times it takes, in a calm, authoritative tone of
voice. When they get nailed by a false assumption about the computer's behavior, tell them their assumption was reasonable. Tell
yourself that it was reasonable. It was.*

■ *Don't say "it's in the manual." (You probably knew that.)*

# About Observing Learning

This story is not about computers but it is about observing learning,
a skill you really want to develop for yourself and incorporate into
your **home learning culture**. I chose it over many that more directly involve computers because it makes a universal point with unusual clarity. And because I want to insist that one can only develop
good learning habits with the computer if one develops them everywhere. And finally because it happened to me while I was writing
this book and shows that even after many years as a "learning
watcher," one can still be caught off guard.

Ian asked me to work with him on building a rather complex model
following the cleverly language-free building instructions that come
with **Lego** sets. I sat next to him on the floor, surrounded by a sea
of unsorted Lego, and watched his work, occasionally carrying out
a request to do a job under his direction—sometimes a physical job
of separating pieces with more force that he had in his five-year-old
hands, sometimes a request to help find a particular piece or to
answer questions like "What's wrong here?" The degree of involve-

ment was sufficient to enhance my enjoyment of spending time with Ian. I liked the fact that I did not have to pretend to be more involved. Building with Lego is pleasurable for me in itself. The kind of difficulties that came up were interesting. And the insights into Ian's developing ways of thinking felt real and important.

The hardest part of the work was finding the right pieces. The first steps were easy enough, since those pieces called for by the plan were either very large or very common. But soon the going became more difficult. Some small and unusual pieces were required, and these were proving hard to find.

Suddenly Ian, who had been looking more and more frustrated, announced that he wanted his excavator, a new toy he had long coveted and recently been given for Christmas. My first misinterpretation was to suppose that Ian was ready to abandon the Lego project in favor of easier play with the excavator. I continued to think this even after he began loading the excavator's shovel with Lego pieces. But it soon became apparent that I was wrong. Ian moved the excavator with its load two or three feet away and began unloading the pieces one by one, saying, "We don't need this one. We don't need this one. We need this one . . . " So the excavator was an element in a larger plan to solve the Lego construction problem by first sorting the pieces to pick out those that would be needed for the job.

An excellent plan, and the first moral of the story is to be careful not to be too quick in judging a child's actions negatively. Very often there is more than meets your eye. (Of course this applies to grown-ups as well as to children, but that's not what we are discussing here.)

But why did Ian need the excavator to do the job? His plan could be described abstractly as moving all the Lego pieces out of the original pile and sorting them one by one into two groups. The process of thinking that brought him to use the excavator is obvious in an intuitive sense if one just tries to put oneself into the place of the young problem solver. Looking at the confusing pile of Legos, the idea begins to come to him to look at them one by one. I believe he had been trying to do this in the jumble but found it impossible. So the next idea is to move them out of the messy pile: Instead of bringing the sorting process to the bricks, take the bricks to the sorting process. How to move them? It so happened that a thing for moving stuff happened to be very present in his mind at the time, so he used the excavator.

It is worth dwelling on how Ian's solution differs from one that you or I might have employed. I think I would have used my hands to take the Legos from the pile and transport them to one of two other places: one place for the ones I could recognize as fitting my needs and another for the rejects.

How does using a truck differ from this? In what way is Ian's solution different from mine?

I call the relevant characteristic *concretization*. But that's just a name. **Jean Piaget** and many other theorists of the concrete have given related but different insights into what might lie behind this process. I recommend a very nonacademic first step towards understanding their ideas. Put yourself in the place of the kid. Try to feel how introducing a familiar, concrete representation might make you feel more confident about the process. Perhaps you might even be ready to say you feel warmer if the representation uses something with which you have positive associations.

Then, of course, bringing the excavator into the Lego work might have resolved a conflict for Ian. He had two new toys to play with; this way he could be playing with both.

I am sure that many parents and some teachers would regard the introduction of the excavator as "childish"—something to discourage. On the contrary, I think that personally meaningful rooting of intellectual work is always an advantage. Even for adults. And one of the great advantages of working with computers is the scope allowed for doing just that.

# Projects

## Me as Kid

Think of this chapter as a minicourse in **technological fluency** for the family. Many ideas that have been mentioned somewhat abstractly in earlier chapters will be concretized here, in step-by-step descriptions of projects.

When I was thinking about writing this chapter, I made a list of all the things I could remember doing with my computer in the last few months. I had no intention of including it here; I just thought that playing with one list of computer activities would help me focus on a way to talk about another list. To my astonishment, I quickly realized that there is very little difference in kind between what I do and what I would recommend to an eight-year-old. Then bit by bit I began saying to myself . . . why eight? What about six? Or even four?

So here is my list. It would be boring and repetitious for me to go through it item by item, showing how the activity can be adapted for people at different ages—or, rather, at different levels of technological fluency. So instead I have selected a few projects for this chapter that will, between them, provide examples of ideas and techniques that are rich enough to allow you to adapt the whole list (and much more) to whatever technical level you choose.

### Thirty Things I Did with My Computer

- I drew with it—figures for a mathematical article.
- I composed a cartoon for the first time in my life.
- I played games—mostly with grandchildren.
- I composed new games, one in collaboration with a grandson.
- I wrote programs in several versions of **Logo**.
- I scratched the surface of learning Java.
- I received and sent a few thousand emails.
- I met some interesting people in cyberspace.
- I enjoyed contact with people I love in five continents.
- I talked with students and friends by video conference.
- I conducted seminars by video conference.
- I spent more hours "surfing" than I like to think.
- I sought, and sometimes found, information I thought I needed.
- I serendipitously found information I hadn't thought of needing.
- I picked up useful tips about my computers and software.
- I bought some books and some software at virtual stores.
- I downloaded free software.
- I got into a political fight in a newsgroup.
- I got better daily news and weather forecasts than TV offers.
- I used a CD-ROM to listen to, and learn about, pieces of music.
- I used an ear-training program (*Claire*) to practice singing.
- I practiced speaking Russian.
- I discovered what a magnet does to a computer screen. (Try it!)

- I modeled a math problem "on screen," then solved it "in my head."
- I built several computer-controlled Lego models.
- I showed off my computer setup and things I've done with it.
- I worked out my flight plan for a trip in a small Cessna airplane.
- I tried out maybe thirty software packages and liked three.
- I downloaded the latest version of Netscape while reading my email while waiting for my turn in a video game while listening to the radio. . . .
- I thought about what I'd *really* like to do with a computer.

# Getting Started

Families that have a recent-model computer equipped with a CD-ROM drive and a high-speed modem will probably find that this chapter is most effectively used as an introduction to hands-on work in conjunction with the CD-ROM that comes with *The Connected Family*. However it is intended to be useful even if you do not have access to any computer at all, or if you feel (as I occasionally do) that you can achieve a better "minds-on" relationship with ideas without "hands-on" support, by imagining what is happening rather than by doing and seeing it.

### Note for Heroic Owners of Vintage Computers

I feel the greatest personal affinity with people who do better things with an old Apple IIe (or Atari or MSX or early-model IBM) than most of what is being done with new Pentiums. If you are one of those people, I hope that the following remarks will help you look with a more sympathetic eye at my decision to couch my ideas here in terms of projects for new computers.

First it does seem fair to use the language and examples most familiar to the greatest number of people. Most people who own computers bought them recently and so own recent models. But more importantly, you are probably less "spoiled" than most of those who started with powerful new machines. You are more used to understanding your machine and deploying ingenuity to squeeze more out of it than its designers ever imagined. As a result you are probably better able to read the spirit (and fantasy) of what I want to say when it is expressed in "their language" than those with newer machines would if it were expressed in yours. A pity, but a fact. I hope this will be made less true by this book.

So, since it is impossible to write a readable book that will give specific suggestions for every type of computer, and since I can't bring myself to write in abstract terms that would apply to all computers, I have chosen to make my ideas concrete by spelling them out as images of what to do with modern machines. I just hope that not too many people will read them in a literal-minded way: The underlying ideas are adaptable and far more general than the examples.

In any case, since the limitation comes from the inflexible nature of the printed book and does not apply to hypermedia, I have set up a Web site and a Resource Guide (at the end of this book) through which a wider range of people can obtain specific information, ideas and even software. I cannot promise that the Web site will be there forever, but I will maintain it for as long as possible and believe that if it is really being used well, others will take up the baton when I no longer can.

This chapter is structured around projects you can do in your family, but I want to avoid giving the impression that the best way to deal with this material is to replicate the projects exactly as they are set out here. These projects are really intended as a context through which you can meet ideas, methods and models that can inspire your own family's activities (individual and collective).

I have chosen to use a minimal number of general-purpose software tools. The major work will be done with just two: a browser for exploring the Internet, and **MicroWorlds**. In addition, some very specific tools will have to be used for special purposes, such as capturing an image. If you have any difficulty with these tools, consult *The Connected Family*'s Web site.

# Guiding Principles

The principles that have guided my choice of projects do not include any attempt to be exhaustive. If there is a "curriculum" to be "covered" it is defined entirely in terms of ideas and attitudes, to the exclusion of anything like a "subject." Indeed one of the powerful ideas of **technological fluency** is that there is no subject to which it cannot be applied. This is not surprising. Fluency in your native language allows you to discuss every possible subject; why should this not be equally true of technological fluency?

The first of three major principles guiding my choice of projects here is that they should encourage attitudes of extension: The best things you can do are those that open doors to further things beyond them. Projects would not be projects—and would be boring—if they did not achieve goals, but the best projects have no final goal. Each time you reach a peak is cause for celebration, but it also lets you see further peaks beyond it so the celebration merges into new challenge. The designers of **video games** have understood the principle of rewarding hard-won achievement by giving players yet more difficult levels of challenge.

A second principle could be called "what's food for the goose is food for the gander." I look at what I do with my computer as a source of ideas about what kids can do with theirs. And the reverse is also true: I look with suspicion on anything made for kids that is too boring to be interesting for me.

A third principle is that a good family computer project must have roots in the **culture of children**; it must feel to a kid like it is connected with the kinds of things that kids do, and in particular with the kinds of things that kids do with computers.

The two best established examples of "what kids do with computers" are playing games and surfing the Net. So my third principle leads me to resist any temptation to say: Don't play games and surf the Net; do this other "educational" thing instead. I would see this as disrespectful of children as well as probably futile. I would also see as disrespectful any attempt to disguise as playing a game or surfing the Net something essentially different that I think kids "ought" to be doing. On the other hand I see it as quite respectful to work with kids on understanding these activities and looking for ways to make them richer in one way or another.

One source of enrichment comes from looking at my own computer activities. I too surf the Net. And I often feel that I am wasting my time. Sometimes I am not even enjoying it. I keep going because of the eating-peanuts principle: Doing it just one more time comes so naturally and seems to have so little cost (whether measured in calories of nut fat, minutes of time or quarters at the game gallery). Other times I am enjoying the surfing as I do it but feel afterwards that the pleasure was not worth the time it took.

My sense that I am sometimes "wasting time" using the Internet actually led me to a project that might be interesting as a family activity. I started a "log" (or a "diary") of my Internet activities. And although I have not been completely disciplined about keeping the diary, it has given me a lot of insight into my own habits (as keeping any diary does) and has led to my making better use of my time and the many sources of information available on the Net.

A special fallout for me of the diary was related to a difference between my use of the Net and what I see many children doing. It would oversimplify the difference to say that I approach the Internet in a purposeful, instrumental way (for example, looking for specific information) whereas children surf "randomly." The line between purpose and serendipity is not as clear cut as that would imply. Yet there is something in this difference. I do think I am more often driven than children are by an immediate need to find certain kinds of information. On the other hand, keeping the diary led me to become more aware that in surfing I often ran into something—a Web site or a piece of information or an idea—that might be interesting to someone I know. This idea has grown into a project that illustrates a more general idea: *The Web is a great source of material for assembling gifts for people we love.* It builds connections in the making and the giving.

For example, someone in my family has a pet turtle and would be delighted to receive as a birthday or Christmas present a collection of pictures, facts and stories about turtles. It so happens that on the Web there are some wonderful sites related to turtles, with excellent graphics and fascinating information that could be used to make a specially tailored turtle book. The gift might be even better and more appreciated in the form of a multimedia show on a CD-ROM or, if the recipient likes the Web, a specially created directory of sites on the subject.

I give this kind of project points for incorporating all three of my principles. The third, because making gifts and surfing the Web are activities that children do and love. The second, because I decided to do it myself without thinking of it as "an activity for children." And the first because implementing the project in a form such as making a multimedia show exercises and develops skills of technological fluency. This is clearly true for a child but has been true for me as well; for example, developing this project led me to make the plunge into image-manipulating software tools that I had meant to learn but never had.

# Surfing for Turtles for Grandma

I asked my friend Judy McGeorge to help me with the preparation of this book by trying out some Web exploration projects. She surfed around and eventually reported that there were some great sites related to turtles.

Judy McGeorge simulated a child—let's call her Joan—who knew that her grandmother was interested in marine sea turtles, and who wanted to put together a birthday present based on what she could find about this topic on the Web. As we go along through a fictionalized version of Judy's search, I shall point to issues that can be discussed with children (on a level adapted to their ages or, rather, level of computer savvy) either during the surfing if it is done collaboratively or afterwards.

The first step in the simulation was to initiate a search by clicking on the Search button provided by the Web browser. This offers you a choice of search engines, which are programs run by different organizations, each with its own approach to gathering and searching through information on different sites in the Web. I hope that by the time you read this someone has produced a search engine whose structure is better matched to the interests of young people, and is even capable of being used by a child who does not yet read or write well enough to navigate with instruments intended for adults. At least one such attempt is being made by a company called MaMaMedia, founded by Idit Harel. (Do a search for the name to see whether it has already come into operation.) In May 1996 Joan had to use search engines that were imperfectly adapted to her needs but still led to interesting results.

Joan chooses a search engine called Yahoo because she likes the name, and she enters the single word TURTLE. After a while a message comes back:

116

## 809 Turtle Sites Found

Yahoo found 809 sites that seem to have a connection with turtles. On the screen a list appears of the twenty-five sites that Yahoo counted as best fitting the description "Turtle." At the bottom of the list is a button to move on to the next group of twenty-five.

This would be a good place to discuss strategies if you were with Joan, though she would probably be too impatient for a long discussion. One strategy would be to scan through all 809 entries before even leaving this page to explore what is out there. This may be a temptation for Planners, who want to evaluate all the options before proceeding. A child probably won't allow you this option. As a middle ground, you might want to print or save a copy of the information found in this group. Choose the command Save [this Page] As . . . under the File menu of your program. The text on this page will be saved to a file you can open later with your word processor. Joan chooses to save two of these pages representing the first fifty turtle choices.

Now Joan is likely to be saying, "C'mon, let's go. I think we should go to *The Almost Amazing Turtle Cam (Meet the Turtles)*."

A click on the text of the title sends Joan's request to her own computer connection, then on to the location pointed to by the link. In this case the address you are headed to is:

http://www.campusware.com/turtles/meet.htm

The browser reveals the programming behind the page in case you are interested, but Joan does not have to pay attention to its form.

When Joan gets to the site, she can see that it was probably made by a kid of indeterminate age, apparently the proud owner of five pet turtles: Tubby, Swimmy, Herbert, Sammy and Fred. The site shows pictures and loving descriptions of each of them. Joan is particularly struck by the remark:

Herbert is the friendliest turtle we have. I named him after a turtle I had when I was a kid. (Actually I named all my turtles Herbert.)

The discovery of this page might inspire Joan to set up her own Web page, but it is a little off-track from the search for something about wild marine sea turtles that will interest Grandma.

So how do we turn around?

Joan has already clicked the Back button found near the top of the screen on the left. This takes us back to the last page we were on before going to visit Herbert. We are back at our list of search choices.

## How Do You Choose?

We could of course go back to the search engine with a more narrowly defined criterion, such as SEA TURTLE. Doing so would give us a far shorter list but would deprive us of two advantages of the fuller list. We would lose some of the fun of just browsing through a lot of choices. We also might miss some valuable sites and the possibility of discussing two interesting issues—one logical and one social.

The logical issue is about how the search engines work. Since they do not really understand either the request or the Web pages they scan, they often miss one that might be very relevant. In this case our attempts to narrow the search would have led the search engines to miss a valuable site without the word "sea" in its name. A page called *Herpmed: Turtles and Tortoises* leads to a lot of other interesting sites and also shows an important aspect of the **culture of the Web**.

An interesting social issue that is very much worth discussing at this stage of the activity is how frequently one can get help in making choices from others who have already been there. The summary information about the *Herpmed* site contains a tip alerting Joan that this site could help her find other sites. It says "Turtle and Tortoise Website Links." Clicking on the *Herpmed* link brings Joan to a page containing links to a number of sites about turtles. These sites turn out to be the kinds that someone like Joan or her grandmother are likely to find interesting.

The existence of sites like this provides an opening to discuss the community spirit of the Internet. There is no central organization, but someone with an interest in turtles took the trouble to create a site that will save others the work that must have gone into selecting eleven excellent sites. Like a cairn found on hiking trails, this page gives direction to those that follow.

Making a site like this to help others is a more sophisticated project that could have served like creating gifts to give purpose to a child's Web surfing.

The text of the *Herpmed* Web site looks like this:

## TURTLE AND TORTOISE - WEBSITE LINKS

### Turtle Trax
❏ An amazing site detailing an epidemic of fibropapilloma among Hawaiian Green Sea Turtles. A must see website!

### Sea Turtle Conservation Website
❏ A wonderful site from France available in both English and French.

### The Tortoise Land
❏ A new and upcoming site from Japan. This is the English version but you can click for the original version. Some subsites still in Japanese but will be translated soon. We particularly enjoyed the 3D modeling and computer graphics of tortoises. Check it out!

### Florida Net Sea Turtle Website
❏ A Website from the Scuba Journal on Florida Net. Marvelous color photos and narratives re Florida's sea turtles.

**Texas A and M Sea Turtle Research Program**
❏ Institute of Marine Biology of Crete

**Dr. David T. Kirkpatrick's Turtle Website**

**The Tortoise Trust**

**Teppo's Turtle Website**

**Slowcoach Tortoise Page**
❏ Slowcoach (get it?) from the U.K. with much info on U.K. and European chelonians.

If you know of any other turtle or tortoise sites to add to this listing please e-mail their location to Steve Grenard grenard@herpmed.com

---

Here, gathered in one place, are pointers to information on research groups and individuals in Hawaii, France, Japan, Florida, Texas, Crete and England, all related by a common interest in turtles. Each can be reached by a click of the button on the name.

If Joan is not experienced enough to say "This looks like a good place to put a Bookmark," this would be a good time for her to learn that Web browsers will allow her to record a Web site address using a simple click, so that another single click will bring her back to it at any time. This saves having to re-enter the whole URL, with its slashes and w's, if she does want to get back. Of course she could hope to find her way there a second time by repeating the entire process, including the search from the beginning, but a little thought and experimenting will show that this is not a very reliable way to go—another good talking point.

"The *Sea Turtle Conservation Website* sounds like it might be a good place to try," observes Joan. With one click of a button she is contacting a computer in France.

Indeed it is a good spot to learn about sea turtles. Joan has found a place which describes the work of experts in the field of turtle research and provides an email link to each. There are links to a Web site in Australia, which describes the Year of the Turtle in the South Pacific, and to the Archie Carr Center for Marine Research in Florida and a turtle project in French Guiana. Workshops, conferences and databases of information about sea turtles are listed. All this information is available in French and English versions.

Here we see the great power of the Web. Just a few years ago, if a child (and her grandmother) wanted to know about turtles, they might have set off for the library. But there was no conceivable way that a few minutes—or even a few hours—of work would have put them in direct communication with the top experts in the field.

## The Turtle Trax Page

Having wandered through sites that were suggested by the *Sea Turtle Conservation Website*, it might be time to come back to the *Herpmed* site. This is the situation that was anticipated by creating the bookmark: All Joan needs to do to return to the site is to pull down on the Bookmark menu and click on the name.

Back on the *Herpmed* site, Joan chooses *Turtle Trax* as the next site to visit.

I hope that when you read this you will still be able to visit the *Turtle Trax* site. For anyone, of any age, interested in sea turtles, this is a special place. There are beautiful photographs of sea turtles and startling photographs of sick turtles, a compassionate discussion of an epidemic afflicting sea turtles in Hawaii, a whole Kidz Korner of activities for children to learn about and have fun with sea turtles, information about six species of marine turtles, stories of the efforts by the research team in Honokowai, Hawaii, to save the turtles and much more.

The *Turtle Trax* page was created by Peter Bennett and Ursula Keuper-Bennett. Again typical of the spirit of much that can be found on the Web is the following note, included as part of their site:

Copyright Information

We, Ursula Keuper-Bennett and Peter Bennett, retain all rights to the text and images contained within *Turtle Trax* except where otherwise noted.

We grant the rights to use any or all of our copyrighted material to anyone who wishes to use it, subject to these conditions:

•You must include a credit acknowledging us as the creators of the material.

•You must not use the material in any manner that is detrimental to marine turtles. We reserve the right to decide whether a particular use is detrimental.

The images contained in these pages are limited in quality by the medium. We will, upon request, make our highest quality images available at no charge to those who intend to use them to further public awareness of sea turtles, or who are trying to raise funds for sea turtle research.

We can now imagine Joan going on to complete her gift project in any of several different forms. The simplest would be to take her grandmother to the best sites she has discovered by using bookmarks. Among many disadvantages of that choice is the time that it takes to download a good image. So instead Joan might choose to create a show on her own computer that will include the pictures, perhaps woven together with her own text and sequenced in her own manner to convey her feelings about turtles and the people who have dedicated themselves to protecting them. Or she might have downloaded pictures from sites like *Turtle Trax* and constructed a book for her grandmother.

# A Bigger Step Towards Technological Fluency

Joan's project goes beyond a level of **technological fluency** that has been acquired by ten million Americans only in one respect: Large numbers of people who have used Web browsers to look into sites as we imagined Joan doing have not taken the extra step of creating their own project. Joan's idea of creating a multimedia show could take very many different forms. Imagine, for example, a gift such as the following:

> Presented with an opening screen with postage-stamp-sized pictures of turtles, Grandmother can click on any one. The chosen picture will enlarge to fill the whole screen and show two small buttons at the bottom. If she clicks on the STAMPS button, the original page will come back. If she clicks on the THREATS button, she will find a page of summaries of situations that are dangerous to turtles. If she clicks on any of these summaries she will see an animated and/or movie sequence, with sound effects representing a threat to turtles and the actions taken by people who are trying to protect them. After each of these she can go back to the THREATS screen or to an EXIT screen that will show her statistics about turtles and end with a turtle swimming up to center screen with an appeal for action.

The actions in this show will be familiar to anyone who has frequented the world of multimedia. What will be novel for most such people is the idea that they and Joan can create this show without taking a course in computer science.

I haven't said what age Joan is or would have to be in order to do this, because it is so dependent on her background and besides, every child is different. I estimate that a large proportion of children growing up in a **family learning culture** that values **computer fluency** would be making that kind of a production by age five or six and some by age four. But if they don't grow into it gradually from the beginning, they might have to be eight or so in order to learn it in a less natural way.

## Warning

The age at which children learn to program—or do anything else—is not a sign of "how smart" they are. Albert Einstein is often cited as a "slow learner" who turned into a brilliant adult. But of course nobody knows what he was really learning. Perhaps a lot more than they saw!

■

# MicroWorlds

Our work up to this point could be done with many softwares. My choice of software for the next phase is more tightly constrained. In fact, in some situations we shall encounter, **MicroWorlds** is the only software I know that can be used nearly as effectively for the particular project. In other cases, other tools would be as good—or even better if judged entirely as special-purpose tools for the individual project. But a subtext of my discussion questions the very idea of judging software tools by their effectiveness in particular contexts. A great deal of harm has been done to the learning environment by using special-purpose software that happens to be "best" for some immediate project in hand.

## Analogy

In carpentry we use a general-purpose hammer to drive many forms of nails, each suitable for a different situation. It is an interesting mental exercise to design special-purpose nails for different jobs and special-purpose devices to drive them—interesting to think about but not something you wish people had done instead of inventing the general-purpose hammer.

■

**MicroWorlds** is an extended version of the programming language **Logo**, which I initiated in the 1960s. It has lots of faults but, taken overall, Logo is still the only language that has been responsibly designed for children to use. Part of what I mean by "responsibly" is that it is a "language for children" only in the sense that such good literature as *Alice in Wonderland, Winnie the Pooh* and *Charlotte's Web* are "books for children." They are "for children" in the sense that they are accessible to children, but they are not "toy books"–they are real books with real literary quality.

I am not inveighing against all uses of special-purpose software tools. My objection is to thinking that there is no other way, or that any other way must be really difficult or only for specialists. For example, in this chapter I talk about using MicroWorlds to make a multimedia show. Most people who know software would think instead of using Hypercard for a simple project within the reach of children, and Hyperstudio or Macromedia Director to do a really professional job. I hope that as you become proficient you will want to try several ways to make a multimedia production. But at least four reasons contribute to my absolute certainty that the best starting point is a general-purpose programming system.

The first reason is a *sine qua non*: You can get to the level of producing your first interesting effects as easily via this route as any other. The belief that rigid special-purpose software is "easier" has no serious foundation. The second is that what you will be learning will be useful in a large variety of other situations. The third is that at each point you will have a wider range of directions to go than you would with a special-purpose software. And finally, you will be in closer contact with the **powerful ideas** that undergird all computational tools.

Education theorists spend a lot of time worrying about what they call the problem of *transfer*: If you learn something in one context, can you use it in another? If you learned to use a word processor on a Mac, will you be flummoxed if you have to use an IBM? The answer is simple: depends on what you actually learned.

Of course the skill won't transfer if what you learned was a mean-ingless ritual like: Push this key, then that key, then wait for the beep. But if you understood the principles, and if you have an attitude of self-confidence in trying and modifying, your old experience will let you find out quickly what to do in the new sit-uation. *Transfer is not something that happens to you. It's some-thing you do.*

---

I have often heard adults respond to the suggestion of a new machine or software package by complaining: "Oh, no! We've only just managed to learn the old one and now we have to learn something new." I have never, really *never*, heard this complaint from kids who were to any serious degree engaged with computers. Invariably their reaction is more like: "Wow, I wonder how to make this one do . . ." and they're off on the search for how to strut their old stuff with the new system and do new things they hadn't done before.

■

The version of MicroWorlds described in this chapter assumes that the user can read and type. But on the book's Web site you will find an "iconic" version made by Sergei Supronov, a researcher at the Institute of New Technologies in Moscow.

# From Consumer to Producer of Point-and-Click Actions

The first purposeful computer act is often pointing and clicking. It is certainly one that can be picked up very early. Click on Grand-ma and she will talk. Click on the postage-stamp-sized picture of a frog and it will be replaced by a full-screen picture. Click on the arrow pointing off the bottom right-hand corner of the page and the next page will appear. Click on the underlined index on the Web site's home page and the index will appear on the screen.

Point and click has become a symbol of a new way to interact with the world. It has acquired its conventions. And it has become part of what children expect from the earliest age. Although it is not always obvious to me what lies behind the emotional force that makes point and click so appealing to a child, it certainly exists.

## A Little Learning Story

The CD-ROM production of *Peter and the Wolf* gives the user a choice of letting the whole story with music run automatically or turning the pages by clicking on an arrow. Six-year-old grandson John first alerted me to a behavior that should have been obvious: The manual drive was much preferred. Pursuing the question led to a very strong statement about why a CD-ROM is better than a videotape even in a case like this, where at first sight I thought there was no "real interaction."

"'Cause you do it!" was the essence of his position.

It is elementary to me that children should experience creating the kind of thing they like to use.

■

Our first scenario is about acquiring this power and giving it to children. We begin by launching MicroWorlds. A first hurdle to using it is so elemental that it has never as far as I know been mentioned in writing about software. When MicroWorlds comes up on screen some people feel a slight shock, not because of anything that it does but because it doesn't do anything at all. Most software for children takes the initiative by doing something, even if just playing music. Most, but not all. A word processor does nothing until you begin to type; a paint program does nothing until you begin to draw with it. But in these cases, at least you know in advance what it is for, what it is waiting for you to do.

MicroWorlds is far more open-ended: You can "tell" it to be like a word processor and let you type, or to be like a drawing program and let you draw. Telling it is not complicated; it becomes a paint program if you click on an icon of a paintbrush, for example. Pretty simple. But *you* have to act first. And we are not really accustomed to that degree of freedom.

So let's start by making it be a paint program, since the icons and language of such programs are rapidly entering the universal **culture of children**. When MicroWorlds puts on its paint program hat, it shows a "palette" of "tools" similar to what you would see (with minor variations) if you had just fired up KidPix or any one of a dozen or more other widely used drawing programs for children. Now you have to choose a tool; the pencil or the eraser and the spray gun are the most common. Choosing means clicking on it. If you are going to draw you need to choose a color and a thickness of line. Do it, and drawing consists of "dragging" the mouse. Where you drag leaves a line of your chosen color and thickness.

One could think of this paint program as a language with its own grammar. "Horses run fast" is a sentence of English, and pen-color thickness is a sentence in the paint programming language. Maybe learning it involves mobilizing children's innate language-learning instincts. Maybe not, but in any case they learn it quickly. Do you want another color? Another line thickness? Eraser instead of pen? Do the intuitive thing and the intuitive result will follow.

No, I did not forget we were going to talk about giving children control of the use of point and click. So far we have seen it used, not created. We needed a warm-up exercise and a context.

Now suppose that you have drawn on the screen in many colors, including red. Let's go on to see what makes MicroWorlds much more than a paint program. When the color is laid down on the screen in ordinary paint programs, it is passive. It doesn't do much. MicroWorlds allows a color to be "hot" or "active." We'll first do this in a way that won't be suitable for a typical five-year-old. When you (or your seven-year-old) have gotten the idea, we'll go back to worry about the little ones.

Double click on the red patch in the palette. A dialog box opens, inviting you to write something. Let's try the word CLEAN.

Click on OK, the universal gesture for telling the box you are done with it. Your screen covered with multicolored scribbling is still there. Click on a blue patch. Nothing will happen. Then try a red patch and—oh my gosh, the screen has been wiped clean.

Don't worry, we didn't lose all our painting. Click on the UNDO icon and it will come back. Let's extend our giving color meaning. Let's make green mean restore. Double click on green. Dialog box opens. Type UNDO. Close box.

Click on any red patch. Screen clears. Click on green to bring it back . . . oh dear, there isn't any green! We cleaned it off! The best-laid schemes of mouse (sorry!) . . . In computer jargon this kind of happening is called a bug, and I strongly suggest using this word rather than "wrong" or "mistake" or "error." Bug has a more positive sound and encourages a more positive attitude. In school if you get something wrong you get a bad grade and that's often the end of it. In this kind of situation, thinking about what actually happened when you tried your little program (for that is what it is) gets you on the track of bringing it closer to what you wanted to achieve.

# Digression: Chasing a Bug . . .

You thought you could make this drawing flash on and off by clicking the mouse on the right places, but you have to think again. What is great here is that *thinking again* leaves you understanding what happened, and understanding what happened leads you to understand how to make something different happen.

Your scheme didn't "just not work." It did exactly what you told it to do. Recognizing the discrepancy between what you actually *told* it and what you *meant to tell* it is a big step towards getting it to "work" and an excellent exercise in formal language.

MicroWorlds allows you a host of ways to deal with the bug. The simplest doesn't change the program but gets around the bug (which is what you have to do most of the time when there is a bug in commercially made software): You can always bring your picture back by painting a new spot of green on the screen and clicking on that! Another way to fix the bug is to use more reasoning, such as: There's no green after the picture was erased, so green was a bad choice of color. If I had chosen white instead of green there would have been no trouble at all—I could just click anywhere on the white screen. So I can fix the bug by attaching the instruction RESTORE to white instead of to green.

A deeper way of thinking could lead one to believe that it is dangerous to use color as the marker for the hot place when the effect of clicking is going to be changes in color. As we shall see soon, MicroWorlds allows you to make a patch of color that will be exempt from the action of CLEAN, or to create screen objects called buttons, which will also be exempt from CLEAN and can be marked with the words CLEAN and RESTORE, or to invent icons to stand for these actions.

Encountering and dealing with the "green bug" is an excellent example of constructionist problem solving. Nobody "gave" you a problem. It came up naturally, as problems do in the course of trying to get something done. And it reinforces a frame of mind that sees such events as the natural path to getting something done. Mistakes are the steps to success, provided you know how to handle them.

# Things to Do with a Click

Although making a doodled picture appear and disappear is not really exciting as a project, I have seen kids (and adults) respond to it as exciting for its promise of control of a process that "prestigious people" do—people like designers of games and CD-ROMs and Web sites and the like. When I introduce kids to this means of control, I move quickly on to show them an extensive range of actions and events that can be controlled. One of these, which resonates with experiences children know well, is clicking somewhere as the computer form of flipping to another page.

In MicroWorlds you create multiple pages simply by pulling down a menu marked Pages, which gives you the option of creating a new page. Do this. Get a blank page. Draw something on it. Now let's change our color instructions: Instead of CLEAN and RESTORE, let's type PAGE1 and PAGE2. We can click on the colors to switch between the pages.

More interesting than simply doodling scribbles on each page is to embark on a more serious project of building a family book, with a page for each member of the family. Looking at some examples of what can be put on each page by means as simple as what we have seen so far will give me the opportunity to introduce the programming concepts that form the core of this little course.

Just what you can do depends on what equipment you have. For example, if your computer has a microphone you can include the family member's voice speaking a message. The MicroWorlds tool kit shows an icon that obviously represents a microphone. Click on it and then point and click on any place on the page. A box will open with the well-known symbols for play, record and stop. Click on RECORD, say the message, click on STOP. Click on PLAY and you will hear your message. Press OK and the dialog box disappears. On the page you now see an icon representing a person speaking. Click in the icon and you hear the message.

Many recent-model computers will have a microphone built in. If yours does not, you should definitely get one. This is an inexpensive piece of equipment that every family computer should have. You can also download sounds from the Internet or buy them on disks or CD-ROMs.

Just as you can import sounds into the computer you can import pictures, and you have the same range of methods. If you just want pictures, not necessarily *your* pictures, you can import huge numbers from the Web using a modem. If you have a CD-ROM drive, you can buy inexpensive CD-ROMs with thousands of excellent and interesting pictures.

If you want your own picture—the equivalent of using the microphone for sounds—the least expensive way is to use a service now offered by photo developers: When you get your roll developed, specify that you want the pictures on a diskette. Next up in cost (and much more fun) is to have a digital camera connected to the computer. I love a little camera called Quickcam, which comes in a black-and-white version for about a hundred dollars. Another route is to buy a video capture board, which will allow you to connect your video camera to the computer and capture still frames or movie clips (which have to be short because they guzzle your computer memory). Both of these methods allow you to have some video conferencing across the Net—an excellent family activity. You can also get still pictures into the computer by using a machine called a scanner, which looks and works like a copier to transfer pictures into files in the computer.

The close similarity between dealing with sounds and images is more than just a practical convenience. It brings you in touch with one of the most **powerful ideas** of digital thinking. Up to the early part of the twentieth century, a sound and a picture were as different as could be. They were handled by different technologies, they were recorded on different media. The development of the "talkies" was the first major step towards bringing them together: Both were recorded as differences in transparency of celluloid film. TV took another step. Both were now transmitted as modulations of "radio waves." But the waves still looked different. It is only with the computer that sound and picture are really reduced to forms that look identical. Both are represented digitally as a long series of 1's and 0's, and there is no way you can tell which is which by looking at them.

Inside your computer, a sound or a picture are reduced to files like any other, for example like the letter you wrote or the record of your tax information. So as soon as you understand how to move files around in your computer, you also understand how to handle pictures, sounds, movies and whatever else you succeed in "getting into the computer." Getting a picture or a sound into MicroWorlds is essentially like getting a text file into a word processor (or into MicroWorlds). Once you have them there instructions in **Logo** will allow you to perform operations on them. Let's suppose we are dealing with a picture. You have brought it into MicroWorlds. The following are examples of operations on the picture that I have seen done by kids of six, seven and eight:

- Make the picture disappear and reappear in response to a click on a color or on a button or on an icon or on the picture itself.

- Make the picture change size; for example shrinking it to stamp size and expanding it to full-screen (or any other) size.

- Make the picture move.

These operations can now be combined into producing actions like:

An airplane flies across the screen, towing a banner on which is written the name JOE or a picture drawn by Joe or a photograph of Joe or all of the above.

In the following project we develop the ideas that lie behind doing these things.

133

# From Writing to Multimedia: Empowering Storytelling

## Jason's IMP (Interactive Multimedia Production)

From the earliest age, Jason was a superb teller of stories. He seems to know by instinct how to use the dramatic gesture, the pause, the shift of stress and tone of speech to play the audience like a skilled musician plays an instrument.

For example, he can breathe life into the simple story that begins "I was walking along a country road by the dim light of a quarter moon." His gestures and expression create an ambiance of tension. "There's a sound, something's moving." Body language conveys the sudden stop, the cautious looking around. "I saw nothing . . ."

But when Jason was asked to write stories at school he was far from being the only kid in his class to find himself unable to transfer to the new medium his oral storytelling skill. When he writes it is plodding, wooden, one word after the other. "I was walking. It was nearly dark. I heard something. I looked. I couldn't see anything. I walked some more. It happened again. Then I saw it was my shadow." He is kept from effectively developing the story by a discomfort with the process of writing, by an insufficient mastery of words to tell a story powerfully without the supports available when he speaks and by impatience with the slowness of his own writing and the ugliness of the best handwriting he has yet learned to produce.

For Jason, MicroWorlds opens new horizons of expressive creativity by allowing him to turn a story into a simple multimedia show. It can be like writing in several ways. He can construct a permanent product that he can show, examine and change. He can even use writing as one element in a larger whole. For example, he can use "real time" to create the tension of walking fast, slowing, stopping in fear, then cautiously moving along. The same sentences that are so dull when written down one after the other gain life when they are flashed on the screen one by one, with an artful sense of timing. This simple expedient enables Jason to use his sense of timing the dramatic pause to create and exploit tension and surprise.

He can do this entirely by managing the appearance on the screen of text and sometimes does so. But why should he impose this restriction on himself? The computer allows him to combine sounds and graphics and animations with the text and, if he wishes, to make events depend on the actions of his audience. A click of the mouse, or, more to his liking, a shout detected by the computer's microphone or pressing a button on a remote controller will make the events go one way or another. In cybertalk, he is now delving into interactive hyper-multimedia. In two or three years' time, kids like Jason will be extending their productions to qualify as virtual realities.

The story of Jason raises two kinds of questions. The nitty-gritty, technical question comes first: How does he make the screen tell a story? Showing how he can do this will lead us to confront a more profound question: How does this skill relate to the skill of writing? Is this activity a diversion that will take Jason away from writing, or is it a bridge that will bring him closer? Or, indeed, as we shall discuss more in Chapter 8, is it the expressive mode of the future and what Jason will really need as he grows up into an increasingly digital world?

## Programming the Show

Start the long journey with a single step: Let's see how to make the words "I was walking on a dark road" appear on the screen at the right time. The following steps anticipate how we learn to think about the process.

■ Step 1: Create a text object.

■ Step 2: Give it a name so we can refer to it later in order to get control over it.

■ Step 3: Embed instructions for the actions to take place in a sequential program.

To create the text object, we look around the MicroWorlds page for something that suggests the process of writing. Sure enough, one of the places inviting a click is marked by the letters "a,b, c . . ." in a way that suggests the function we want. Click on it. Point to a place on the screen and again do the obvious. It may need three or four tries. But you will soon get a feel for the way this icon creates a "text box"—a rectangular space with a blinking cursor that invites you to enter text. Do so. For example, type "I was walking on a dark road . . ." in the text box. Underneath this main box are small dialog boxes asking for your decision about various relevant matters such as "Do you want the text to appear with a frame around it?" At this stage we follow a good prescription for dealing with the quirks of computer systems: If you can't see the point of it, ignore it. (But keep it at the back of your mind!) Because MicroWorlds is a (relatively) well-made system it will allow you to do this and instead of doing nothing because you didn't tell it what to do, it will follow a course that is important enough in the world of software to have a special word: *default*. In computer jargon (CJ) the default action means that action which is done when nobody says to do anything else.

Some software sits and blinks at you (or not even as much as blinks) until you do something. Occasionally this is forced by the fact that there simply is no possibility of a default. Most of the time, though, it comes from poor thinking or poor design. Do take the trouble to reflect on the fact that this use of defaults is not just a frill: It is a powerful design feature that opens the door to powerful modes of learning by adhering to the principle, "Don't just sit there, do something." Of course this design feature and this mode of learning are most effective when the system is designed to do something in turn according to the complementary principle: "Don't just be right or wrong, be informative."

■

In earlier sections we learned a few words of Logo. The first were the commands CLEAN and RESTORE, referring to drawings we made on the screen. In this context we need to do something similar to text we have written in text boxes. Among several ways to achieve this are the commands HIDETEXT and SHOWTEXT.

To try these out, click on the space at the bottom of the MicroWorlds page we called the command center. Type HIDETEXT and follow this with return, which is the universal code for telling the computer "now do it." The text box will vanish. Then type SHOWTEXT. When you hit return, the text comes back.

We are moving towards being able to tell a story on the screen in a dynamic way by controlling when and where words will appear. But a story with one sentence is not much of a story. Jason's idea is to create a show in which:

> The words "I was walking on a dark road . . ." dissolve into view and stay there for a while to the accompaniment of gentle music. Then a sudden sound is heard and the words "I thought I heard and saw something" appear more abruptly, in a sharper font. Music changes to a more ominous drumbeat . . . and so on.

As a principle of project management you can't do everything at once, so the next step could be to forget about the music for a while, make three text boxes and worry about how to control them.

We go though the same process we used for making the first, entering the appropriate words in each. We might as well position them so that they appear at different places on the screen.

We know the commands SHOWTEXT and HIDETEXT, but don't yet know how to address the commands to a particular text box.

At this point we might recall that when we created the text boxes we were given the opportunity to name them. Now we see why! If the boxes have names, we can refer to them separately and so have greater control.

This idea of always "naming" the things you make is a deep feature of computational systems and something that we eventually must come to do instinctively. But in this respect MicroWorlds is a (again, relatively) well-behaved system (as systems go) because it offers a "soft entry" to this habit. First, if you don't give a name, it will give a name for you whenever it can instead of complaining or freezing up. In this case look at your text boxes and note that they have names: Under each of them is written something like text1 or text2. Not very elegant names, but we can use them all the same to control the appearance and disappearance of text on the screen by instructions like:

TEXT1, SHOWTEXT

TEXT1, HIDETEXT

TEXT2, SHOWTEXT.

If we don't like these names we can change them. Beginner kids will probably want to do this by choosing the tool whose icon looks like a scissors and whose effect is to delete objects such as text boxes. Using this tool they can start again, positioning the box where they now know they want it and giving it the name they want. *Let them.* If you happen to know there is an easier way, keep it for later. What might seem easier to you might not at all seem better to a child who has not yet been indoctrinated with the importance of "efficiency."

MicroWorlds actually offers several ways to modify the name, position and other attributes of an object that has already been created. The one that will prove most useful is doing a "shift-click" on the text box, which will reopen its dialog box, offering you the opportunity to enter whatever name you like. It could be JOE or MARY or simply XYZ, but it's best to use meaningful names. In this case we might pick ONE, TWO and THREE, referring to the three sentences that will appear in that order in our show.

---

One of the important contributions of programming as an intellectual discipline is revealing to children the power of the idea of naming in science and mathematics as well as in languages and cultures.

■

Only one more step is needed to make a first version of the show: We need a way to make the three boxes appear in sequence at just the right intervals and the right places.

We can do this "by hand," running each of the three instructions in turn at the right time. But to automate the process we need something more like the popular concept of a computer program: something that will make things happen in the right order. If this "something" were simply issuing the command to the three boxes to appear in sequence, the computer's idea of "one after the other" would look to the human eye like appearing simultaneously! An almost self-explanatory new word of the Logo language–wait– allows us to articulate the instructions as:

ONE, SHOWTEXT

WAIT 40

TWO, SHOWTEXT

WAIT 20

THREE, SHOWTEXT.

What is not self-explanatory about the meaning of *wait* is what the numbers mean. I'll whisper to you that they are tenths of a second, but I'd do something different if I were talking to a child or if you were next to me. I'd say: Try any number! If you don't like it change it. Doing this often enough is the best way to learn what a tenth of a second is, and in doing so enrich one's idea of what "a second" and "a tenth of" mean.

But how do we make the little program run? **Logo** transforms this question into a slightly different one, more rooted in intuitive everyday knowledge: How can we make (or "define") a new command in Logo that will cause the sea quake of events to happen?

A good way to solve many computer problems (and others as well) is to do some wishful thinking. Let's pretend we have already solved the problem and see what happens to us. Solving the problem would mean that we now have a Logo command that would do the job. Since we imagine having invented it, we can choose the word for it: Let's say we want the command to be STORY. This would mean that typing STORY in the command center and pressing "return" will make it happen.

Of course it won't, since we have only imagined defining STORY for the computer so that the process would begin. We don't even know how to go about doing it. But in the spirit of wishful thinking, let's type STORY to see what happens. *Very often when you don't know what to do, doing something will tell you more than just sitting there!*

Computers are seldom completely predictable so I cannot be sure what will happen. What I hope will happen if you try this is that you will read on the screen: "I don't know how to STORY." So, if the machine doesn't know how to STORY, let's tell it. We do this by typing the following into a place offered by MicroWorlds with the label Procedures. What we are giving it is in fact a procedure for an action we want it to know by the word STORY (which we are using here as an imperative verb intended to mean: tell the story about the scary walk. . . .).

This is what we type, except for the parts to the right of the arrows that I have added as explanation:

TO STORY <— This tells the computer that we are about to tell it how to
STORY.

ONE, SHOWTEXT

WAIT 40

TWO, SHOWTEXT   These are the instructions that make up the procedure.

WAIT 30

THREE, SHOWTEXT.

END <— This tells the computer that we are done.

## Enriching STORY with Sound Effects

Jason had in mind from the beginning to do something much more complex than simply showing three sentences. But a good mentor or wise adult collaborator might have suggested: "Let's do one part of it first." The point is that with a minimum of time and effort Jason has made something that actually works! So the construction process can always go from one working system to another more interesting, often more complex one.

Let's say that in this case the next element to introduce is sound effects, though of course the order could easily have been reversed. We could have made the sound effects first and then added the words. An appropriate sound effect for the opening shot, walking quietly along, could be cheerful music. Let's look at some of the ways it could be obtained. They all come down to getting the music in digital form into the computer and giving it a name—I'll choose SOFTLY. When this has been done we'll go back to the procedure TO STORY and replace the second line by the instruction SOFTLY, so that instead of waiting and doing nothing the computer will cause the music so named to be played.

I mention three ways to get the music into the computer:

The icon that looks like a microphone is a tool to record sounds through the computer's microphone. If you click on this tool, icons unmistakably like the controls of pre-computer recording devices will prompt you to click to start and stop recording, and then you'll be asked to give the sound segment a name. Between clicking RECORD and clicking STOP you could be whistling or humming or singing the tune you want. Or playing it on an instrument or whatever.

Instead of the microphone icon, you could have chosen an icon marked with conventional symbols for musical notes. You would then have seen on the screen a representation of a keyboard. Play the tune you like. You can take the time to pick out the notes; this is a digital world so it can ignore the tempo you use and play back the notes at the tempo you tell it to use. And if you are not yet ready to specify a tempo, it will use a default tempo. And of course you can edit the notes as if you were using a word processor. In the end, as usual, you will give the tune a name (in this case SOFTLY), click on OK and try your procedure.

A third way to get sound is to copy it from a CD. The details of doing this are left to our CD-ROM, since if your computer can't read the CD-ROM you can't make the copy. The interesting point is not how to do it but the fact that when you have made a copy of the sound from a CD you can treat it just like a sound made in any of the other ways. Bits are bits wherever they came from.

## Making Motions

Now suppose that Jason wishes to make his story more graphical by putting in it a figure representing him as he walks along. This might make you think that this activity is becoming more like animation than like writing a story, more like Walt Disney than like a writer. But such objections beg the big question. Undoubtedly the digital world blurs the line between what used to be separate arts and separate media. But is this a good development, a bad development or simply an inevitable development? We can only know by following through to see what it is like, and then being sufficiently involved with it to exert our own taste and judgment. My own personal view is that working in the combined media allows a child to focus on the essential features of narration, drama and storytelling and will enhance the ability to work in any of them.

But here we should be talking about how to do it. How can Jason make an animated figure walk across the MicroWorlds screen? Once more the powerful but sometimes scary aspect of MicroWorlds comes out in the fact that there is no single way to do it. I shall concentrate here on what I consider to be the best entry point to dealing with motion, not only as an element of artistic creation but also as it comes up in mathematics and science, leaving for a later chapter a chance to touch on other approaches.

Our tool for creating motion is an example of a computational object I created nearly thirty years ago that has come to be known as the **Logo Turtle**. In MicroWorlds, it appears as a rather schematic drawing of a turtle on the screen. Its special qualities are contained in the commands it can "obey" when these are expressed in Logo—or for very young children, as icons.

If one gives the turtle the command FORWARD 1, it moves forward one tiny "turtle step." The command FORWARD 100 will make it move a hundred times as far. To produce continuous motion we instruct the computer to take a small step over and over again. For sophisticated users this is done by giving a command like FOREVER [FD 1], while beginners can get the same result simply by clicking in a box marked "Many Times." The bigger the step the faster the motion: FOREVER [FD 3] will produce a motion with three times the speed as FOREVER [FD 1]. Exactly how this works is far easier seen than said; if you look at the explanation on the CD-ROM you will find it quite believable that four-year-old children are able to do it.

So with these simple commands it is possible to create a simple motion. From there to go on to more interesting motions, I would show a child two routes.

First, the turtle can be made to carry a shape. As with sounds, it does not matter one bit (the pun is intended) where the shape came from. You can draw it with the paint tools or you can import it from a scanner or take it from one of many collections of pictures that can be bought on CD-ROMs (or on floppy disks if you don't have a CD-ROM drive) or you can "grab" it from a Web site. The easiest way to get a feel for how to use the turtle to make the simplest animation is to use one of the shapes that comes with MicroWorlds.

As usual there is an icon which will open up a collection of shapes if you click on it. You'll find it easily enough. Then there are two ways you can "tell" a turtle to carry that shape. Click on the shape—let's say the airplane—and then on the turtle. The turtle shape will vanish and be replaced by the airplane. Now if you order the turtle to move, what you will see is the airplane moving across the screen.

The other way is to give an instruction. To do this you need to name the shape, just as we needed to name text boxes and sounds or, as in this case, know what name someone else gave it. Double click on the shape in the shape palette. As usual a dialog box will open up, offering you tools to change the shape if you so wish, and showing you the space in which a name can be written. The name already there is PLANE. You can leave it or change it. Let's leave it. Now the instruction SETSH (short for SETSHAPE) "PLANE will have the same effect as the clicking we did earlier. You will wonder what the quotes are doing there; there is a logical reason for this, but what you should really do is postpone even thinking about it until you have had some experience with Logo. You'll find explanations on the CD-ROM, on the book's Web site and in a number of books and videos about **Logo** mentioned in the Resource Guide.

That was the first of three ways to make motions more interesting. It doesn't change the movement but does make what moves more interesting. The second way I'd show a child to make the motion more interesting is to get control over its direction. The instruction FORWARD 100 makes the turtle move in the direction it is heading. Other instructions make it change its direction. You can guess two of these (and that's all you need, though there are more when you want to exert more subtle kinds of control). The instruction RIGHT 90 makes the turtle turn right ninety degrees. LEFT 45 makes it turn left forty-five degrees. And of course using other numbers as inputs to the commands LEFT and RIGHT will do what you expect.

With these instructions we can really control the movement of the turtle (and of whatever shape it has become). A fun way to get a sense of this is to create two buttons with associated instructions LEFT 90 and RIGHT 90. Set the turtle in continuous motion. Drive it around the screen by clicking on these buttons. Paint obstacles. Drive the turtle between them.

## Back to Jason

We have abandoned Jason. But that's the way to learn to do things with computers. We helped Jason bring his project to the point where he wanted to make a figure walk, stop and start again, perhaps changing its gait from cheerful in the first part to cautious in the third. To do this we had to leave the project, get the hang of making things move and then get back to the project. We are now beginning to see the elements of an interesting little show using texts, sounds and moving graphics. It is only the beginning, but it is already enough to make clear a crucial aspect of **computer fluency**.

objects such as turtles, buttons, text boxes and others I have not had occasion to mention here. Of course there are striking differences. On the negative side, a major difference is that these pieces exist only on a computer screen. You can't actually pick them up. But with this more ethereal existence come three great advantages. There is no such thing as running out of them! With a flick of the mouse you can always make another copy. There is no such thing as having a situation in which there is a part that doesn't quite do the job you want. These can always be changed. They are made out of software and can be remade as you want them. And finally they are active. You can make them with behavior as well as with shape and color. All this will become clearer as we go through making a game.

MicroWorlds is like Lego in another respect also. It allows work to proceed in the two **styles**–Planner and **Bricolage**–discussed in Chapter 5. The style of the Planner is to design it all in detail in advance and then implement the design. The style of the **Bricoleur**, however, is closer to the way we build most original Lego constructions. You pick up a few pieces and start putting them together according to some very general idea of where you are going. Or perhaps without any idea. As you add pieces your idea becomes clearer. Eventually you might throw away the pieces you used to get going in this doodling style. But the essential point is that the idea was allowed to evolve. One could say that the idea was plastic and could be molded and shaped.

So we start with a vague idea that we'll make a game something like Pacman. Since we are acting here in a Bricolage spirit, we probably don't care to copy the classic game exactly. And even if that is our eventual goal, we might start by making our own game in the same genre to get a feel for this kind of work.

You might remember, if you have been around that long, that Pacman, which was a popular game in the early eighties, was designed specifically to get away from the model of video games based on shooting. A game based on eating would, it was hoped, be more attractive to peace-loving people in general and draw more girls into the video-game market. It succeeded to some small extent in each of these goals.

In case you don't remember, Pacman is a screen creature shaped like:

The V is a mouth which opens and closes in an eating action. In fact Pacman does eat little cookie objects lying on the screen, and the goal of the game is to eat as many of these as possible before being eaten by a ghost, a third kind of object in the Pacman game.

Pacman and the ghosts move in the confines of a maze. The player controls the Pacman, hoping to follow a strategy that allows the Pacman to eat many cookies and avoid the ghosts for as long as possible.

Now in my best **Bricolage** style I want the process of making a game to be like building towers from blocks or Lego. Right from the beginning we have something that works. Then we'll add to it, push it around, and remold it to grow into something more complex and more like Pacman.

How do we start? I could decide to start by making a Pacman shape that opens and closes its mouth under my control. Or I could decide that I want a maze through which I can guide a moving object. But the simplest way to start is to *use what we've got* (a very fine slogan!), and what we have is a pair of buttons that drive a turtle around the screen. That's a start. We also played with driving the turtle between obstacles in our last project, which is in fact very much like a maze. So turn the question around! What do we *not* have?

One answer is that, although up to this point we may have tried to keep the turtle off the obstacles, in a real game it should simply be impossible for the turtle to cross the wall of a maze or whatever kind of obstacle we might place on the screen.

How do we do this?

We have already encountered the technique to do this in an easy way. Choose a color to be the obstacle color and give it an instruction to do something whenever a turtle comes on it. What instruction depends on what kind of game you want. One extreme view would make the game end if ever a turtle (which will eventually mean Pacman) goes on the black. There could be a horrible noise, followed by the popping up of a text box with the words GAME OVER, followed by stopping everything with the instruction STOPALL.

That was pretty brutal. A gentler response to the turtle getting on the black could simply be to make it step back. If the turtle is doing FORWARD 1 repeatedly to keep moving, and if the color black is programmed to issue the instruction BACK 1, the turtle simply won't go onto the black. Anything black would become a real wall. So let's decide to do that. Now we can draw a maze and have something a little closer to a real game.

In Pacman the excitement came from having ghosts that would destroy the Pacman if they got to it. It should be clear how to start making one of these. We need another turtle. Easy. Yes, you guessed, there is an icon (it happens to show a turtle hatching out of an egg) that responds to a click by hatching another turtle.

It's probably time to dress the turtles as Pacman and a ghost so that we know which is which. We might also give them different names, say, Pacman and Ghost. Well, we know how to give them shapes, and we give them names just as we gave names to text boxes: Double click on the turtle and fill in the name you want. So let's suppose that it is done and go on to think about how the ghost chases the Pacman. Now I could tell you a new command in Logo to use for this. But the time has come to talk about how you can find out.

There are several ways. One is: Ask someone. If nobody around knows, remember you have a computer with a modem and access to the Net. Try to locate somebody who shares your interest! Two is: Browse in the list of all the Logo commands until you find one that sounds like it might do the job. Then try it. Three is: Browse through the collection of projects on the CD-ROM and maybe pick up a clue about how someone else did it. Four is: Read a book. Whichever route you follow you'll either find a way to do it or maybe modify your game so that you know how to do what it needs. (I hope you don't just give up!)

The simplest of several ways you might find is the command TOWARDS, which you use like this:

Ghost, TOWARDS "Pacman <— This makes the ghost head towards Pacman.

Now if there were no obstacles, the ghost would chase the Pacman wherever you drove it. If its speed is set higher than Pacman's, it would catch up. If lower or equal, it wouldn't.

This is probably enough for you to get the point. We can weave the games to become more and more complex and interesting, all the time having a game that does something! On the CD-ROM you'll find a collection of variants to examine and see samples of many directions to go. Browse through them. You'll quickly pick up enough techniques to make very different games.

Oh, one thing should be done here. What happens if the ghost catches Pacman? Browse again at the commands and you'll surely find one with the bizarre spelling seen in this instruction, with funny punctuation that you will quickly understand if you use it a little.

WHEN [TOUCHING? "Ghost "Pacman] [Print [Game OVER] STOPALL]

I stop, leaving you to contemplate that strange statement.

The essential point is that we have here a project made by additions, each of which is simple enough to do in one session. Reward comes soon enough to keep motivated—you don't have to embark on something that will take weeks before there is anything worth having. But the longer you keep at it the more you have. Whoever becomes hooked on this—and lots of kids and even some parents do—will eventually have a product of professional standard that can be shown off and even used by others.

# School

## Don't Be Shy: Go to School

Like "bread" suggests "butter" so "computer" suggests "fast." They work fast, they change fast and they have quickly brought change to many sectors of human activity.

But not to School.

Is this a case of the irresistible force meets the immovable object?

Despite frequent predictions that a technological revolution in education is imminent, School remains in essential respects very much what it has always been, and what changes have occurred (for better or for worse) cannot be attributed to technology. Why is this? Should parents be concerned? And if they are, what can they do about it?

The first question is obviously the hardest. In this chapter I'll tell you what I think without expecting full agreement, as there is obviously room for many opinions not only about why School has not changed more radically, but even about whether it ought to.

My purpose in introducing this discussion is not to convince you, but to challenge you to think about this big question as a means to clarifying smaller but more immediate questions about getting better schooling for your children.

Where there is absolutely no room for different opinions is the second question. More parents ought to take more interest in the computer policies of schools their children attend! Of course some do. In fact in the early days of microcomputers, many computers found their way into schools entirely because of parents—acting individually, working in parent-teacher associations or persuading their employers to donate computers. Today there are many other roles for parents, and I am frequently saddened by noticing how many parents who pay great attention to using the computer to enhance the **learning culture** at home give no serious attention to how well this is being done in their children's schools. Many are scarcely aware of what the schools are doing. Many who take the trouble to find out are reticent about interfering.

This is a mistake. From the narrowest point of view of concern for your children, you ought to keep tabs on what is happening and assert yourself in helping it get better. From a broader social point of view, the special knowledge and insight you are gaining through your home experience can be used to help others. From a political point of view, the way computers are used—or not used—to advance education may have important consequences for the future of the nation and of the world, as well as for you and your family.

There are many immediate ways you can not only influence the school but actively help it. Here are some examples (starting with the simplest and easiest) of the kind of actions I have seen:

- A mother observing her daughter laboriously write an assignment by hand says: "Why don't you use the computer?" Response: an irritated "that's not allowed." After six months the mother can no longer stand watching the frustration and speaks to the teacher, only to learn that the teacher justified the rule against computers by the expectation that parents would be upset if their children didn't practice handwriting.

■ A parent who thinks the work being done in the computer lab is too mechanical asks why they don't do projects like those you saw in Chapter 6. A teacher gives a weary response: "I don't have time to learn, and besides I can't manage a whole class doing that kind of work." One can sympathize with the teacher. But some parents have gone further by taking up the challenge. In a small town a concerned parent mobilized a group of friends to help in a variety of ways, depending on their knowledge and schedules. One was able to run a workshop to help teachers learn more about computers, several offered to drop in to help with computer class, others who did not have free time during school hours offered to serve as on-line consultants. In St. Paul, Minnesota, the 3-M Corporation freed up their engineers who wanted to work in schools for an afternoon a week. Numerous parents have raised money to buy extra computers or pay for running a workshop. In a very small town near where I live, public donations have brought in more than $40,000.

■ School boards have been influenced by relentless lobbying by parents.

Perhaps you are reticent because you fear that intrusion would be resented and that in any case you don't know enough about computers in schools. I can reassure you on both scores. Far from resenting intrusion, most teachers who believe in the use of computers would welcome help and support from parents who share their beliefs. Many would welcome an ally in their struggle with administrators (or even fellow teachers) who do not. And besides, if your interest is resented this means something is very wrong, and all the more reason why you have to do something about it.

As for whether you know enough to have an opinion I feel I must reiterate that *you know more than you think you do*! Common sense combined with your experience of your own home computer learning culture provide a solid foundation of understanding. On this it will be easy to build enough perspective on the computers-in-schools movement to decide what questions to ask and what suggestions to make when you go, as I hope you will, to see the key people in the school.

Apart from your children's teachers, there may be others, perhaps a specialized computer teacher or computer coordinator or even the principal, who might be interested in talking with you if you show real interest and especially if you can offer to help even in small ways. A little sleuthing may be needed to find other parents with an interest in the school's computer policy. On the other hand you may find that a computer teacher who is frustrated by the school administration is looking for allies and can immediately put you in touch with the parents who are active on these issues. A bonus for joining a network of local people might be finding new friends for your children who share their kind of interest in computers.

# Images of Change

My statement that School has not essentially changed would be challenged by many educators—certainly by all **ostriches** but even by many who are trying hard to envisage a very different future. For a sensible discussion I need a scale of change, running from microchange to megachange. At the low end of the scale I place such "reforms" as using a word processor for writing assignments and on-line searches for research assignments. These are so minimal that anything short of universal implementation in a country as rich as the U.S. is a national scandal. The high end of my scale is harder to define. The next section helps give a sense of what megachange in education should be like.

Of course I do not suggest that we run out waving banners and demanding megachange tomorrow. Microchange is meant to represent the end of the scale that should be implemented now. Megachange is meant to represent an ideal that gives direction to smaller changes we can strive for right away.

---

**SA (School Administrator):** Your microchange has a megaprice. We'd have to buy hundreds of computers.

**Me:** Well, so what? You could do it for an increase of one percent in the cost of school.

**SA:** What nonsense! How do you figure that?

**Me:** Your average spending per student per year over the next five years will be $7,000. You could buy very adequate computers in big bulk for well under $700 each. Amortized over ten years, this comes to $70 per year, or one percent of $7,000. So you could give *every* student a whole computer for a one percent increase in your total cost. And this calculation is a wild overestimate of cost. You could achieve a significant change with a computer for every two students. (Not that I recommend that, but just to make my rhetorical point.) And if this were done on a national scale with competitive bidding, someone in the industry would certainly produce a $400 computer.

**SA:** I never heard an argument so full of holes. How can you say "amortized over ten years"? Long before then they'll all be obsolete. Even now a computer you could buy for $700 is far from the best.

**Me:** That's like saying let's walk barefoot if we can't buy a new Cadillac every two years. You can't be seriously saying that kids should write with pencils if we can't afford to buy them the latest Pentium computer.

**SA:** OK, so we'll use old computers. They'll break down and it costs $70 an hour to get a serviceman.

**Me:** Now we are getting somewhere. When I talk about mere *microchange* I do not mean simply injecting computers into an otherwise unchanged school. The students would also learn to *understand* computers. Those who are interested will learn to repair them and learn a great deal more (including a sense of social responsibility) in the process.

**SA:** But we'd have to change curriculum and let teachers learn new things!

**Me:** Now we are really getting somewhere.

■

A LEARNING STORY

# The School of the Future—Images and Metaphors

Imagine a party of time travelers, among them a group of surgeons and a group of school teachers, who came from the last century to see how things are done in our days. Think of the bewilderment of the surgeons when they find themselves in the operating room of a modern hospital! The nineteenth-century surgeons can make no sense at all of what these strangely garbed twentieth-century people are doing. Although they may be able to see that a surgical operation of some sort is being performed, they are unlikely to figure out what it is. The rituals of antisepsis, the practice of anesthesia, the beeping electronics, even the bright lights are utterly unfamiliar. Certainly they would not be able to help.

How different the reaction of the time-traveling teachers to a modern classroom! These teachers from the past are puzzled by a few strange objects, they are shocked by the styles of clothing and haircuts, but they fully see the point of most of what is happening and could in a pinch even take over the class. They disagree among themselves about whether the changes they see are for the better or for the worse.

I use the parable as a rough and ready calibration of extent of change. Some areas of human activity have undergone megachange in the wake of the growth of science and technology. Medicine, telecommunications, entertainment and transportation are among them. School is a notable example of an activity that is not. One cannot say there has been no change in School; of course there has. The point of the parable is to give me a way of saying, "Yes, School has changed . . . but not all that much," and so permit me to pose the question, "Is School susceptible to megachange?"

One might argue that my comparisons with surgery and telecommunications are illegitimate. The latter are essentially technical acts while learning is essentially a natural act like, say, loving or eating. Technology might provide the means to express love, but words of affection spoken into a telephone and relayed through satellites in space have the same meaning as words whispered directly in the ear; the concept of megachange simply doesn't apply. Similarly one might argue that the act of eating is recognizably the same whether the food is cooked in a microwave oven, over an open fire or not at all.

The suggestion that School, too, is simply not susceptible to megachange is supported by the uncanny robustness of its dissemination through the world. I have sat on the grass in Northern Pakistan in the shadow of the Himalayas, among children in a "school" whose only furniture was a chalkboard on an easel and whose only building a bare shelter into which everyone would scurry when the rain fell. The material setting was ever-so-different from anything you might see in an American city, but what was happening was recognizably School. Educators debate the merits of the Japanese and the American systems of schooling. But sitting at the back of a classroom in Osaka, I was overwhelmed by the thought that an extraterrestrial anthropologist would certainly be more impressed by the similarity than the difference.

I have also sat in classrooms with computers on every desk and wondered whether it would take the time-traveling teachers an hour or just five minutes to move from initial surprise to a sense that nothing much had changed after all. Such images bolster the sense of inevitability and naturalness of the concept of School as we have known it.

I have often told a version of this story to audiences of educators. Most find it rather abstract: Yes, they understand that I'd *like* the time-traveling teachers to be amazed and bewildered, but they don't have any concrete idea of *what* might do that. But often one person pipes up with: "I know what it could be—I see a little of it in my own family! It would be like kids learning by roaming the Internet in search of ideas and information, participating in cross-national environmental projects and learning a foreign language by communicating in it. Extend those images a little and you *would* blow the minds of the time travelers."

When the others ask me: "Is that what you mean?" I feel comfortable saying that this is going in a good direction, although real megachange will come only when most learning is taking place in the course of carrying out challenging projects lasting weeks, months or years. Here digital technology has a double role: As a material (or a medium), it lends itself to more complex and sophisticated projects than were previously within the reach of children. As an information and communication channel, it allows children to get access to knowledge when they need it instead of when a curriculum says they should get it. This shift makes nonsense of the idea of a lockstep curriculum and, in fact, of the idea of segregating children into grade levels. Indeed, it makes nonsense of the accepted image of School.

# Will School Do It?

I am frequently admonished for being optimistic about far-reaching change in our education system. Some friends and colleagues even express puzzlement by such comments as: "But how can you of all people be optimistic when you have written so forcefully about the resistance to change in education and about how badly schools use computers?" Sometimes when I attend a school board meeting, which I occasionally do as an observer, or visit schools and see what they are doing, I have a fleeting doubt myself. But if I walk into a computer lab and find that it is one of the ten or twenty percent of such places that still allow their students to use the computers in a personal, expressive way, a few conversations with students quickly send the doubt packing.

The word "still" in the previous sentence might have caught your attention. It reflects a pattern of backward motion in the history of the computers-in-schools movement that you ought to know about if you want to participate effectively in its future—whether you do this for the benefit of your own children or whether you have the time and inclination to help bring learning opportunities to those from less privileged families. The short version of this history is a story of pendulum swings between heights of visionary optimism for change and depths of plodding resignation to business as usual. During the upswings, the tendency has been for computers to be used innovatively; during the downswings, conservatively.

In the past the swings have been associated with waves of new technology. A first round of great enthusiasm in the early sixties was a response to the computer itself. This had subsided by the seventies, when an even bigger and more romantically visionary swing followed the emergence of microcomputers. In schools this upswing reached a peak in the early eighties, when "personal and expressive" uses of computers were dominant in those few schools that had computers. As the eighties wore on, the use of computers became routinized and in many schools was molded into one more ordinary school subject no more exciting than the others and taught in the same traditional way. Now, in the late nineties, a new wave of even greater, and no less romantic, enthusiasm is fueled by the excitement associated with images of networks and information highways and cyberspace.

It remains to be seen exactly what will happen to this wave. Will it be another case of what goes up must come down? I am sure that much of the technocentric hype we are hearing now about revolutionary consequences of wiring schools will soon burst like a big bubble. A computer wired to the Internet in every classroom is much better than nothing, but it's a pitiful microstep towards real change. At the same time I am solidly convinced that this time the upswing is irreversible. A more balanced view of how computers can contribute to educational change will develop, and while its details cannot be predicted, there are many signs that this time we are in it for the long haul.

Skeptics of the possibility of change in schools often recall that it is now a hundred years since the American philosopher and educator John Dewey wrote his persuasive books criticizing the way schools teach and proposing the new methods that became known as progressive education. Nobody has refuted Dewey or proved him wrong—in fact nobody can, since he was very obviously right on the whole. Yet the initial excitement about progressive education faded away, and most schools that adopted progressive methods diluted them down to become window dressing for doing things in very much the same old way. Then there was the Swiss philosopher-psychologist-educator **Jean Piaget**. He is studied by every student in every education school, but you need a mental microscope to detect his influence in schools. The fact is that School has been extremely resistant to change. Why should this time be different?

# Three Forces for Change

The prospects for change in School are different today because for the first time there are forces for change with real fire power. Dewey had to fight his case with philosophical ideas. No match for an institution as solidly rooted as School. Today there are at least three forces whose motives may not be as clear or as pure as Dewey's, but each of them is far more powerful as a social force than any philosophical idea. I list them in ascending order, ending up with what I consider the purest as well as the strongest.

### The first force is a powerful industry.

Big corporations have always had huge clout in education. But the biggest of these, the textbook industry, has been in the past (and mostly still is) a force against too much change. Today an altogether different alliance of forces associated with advanced technology and with new media is looking at the education market with hungry eyes. And this time it is in the interests of the big corporations to do it differently.

It is significant that there is a force for change in education that is not based on educational ideas: The computer manufacturers have a strong interest in getting computers into schools no matter how they are used. But computers that are brought in even for conservative reasons (or simply mindlessly) create opportunities in the schools for significant and even radical change. Other corporations are investing large sums of money in developing new curriculum ideas. Although none of these has yet had a substantial impact, there is no doubt that one or more of them eventually will. Thus, for the first time, a truly powerful force is on the side of change in education.

Of course the role of industry in determining the direction of change in education has its problematic side. I see serious danger in concentrating influence over education in the hands of any organization that is not publicly accountable. However the force is there and cannot be wished away, no matter how much we fear it. Its positive side is that it will contribute to breaking the resistance to change. It is even possible for the negative side to become positive if it serves as an incentive for the development of a "learners' consumer movement" led by parents and others whose primary interest is in democratic social values.

The next two stories will give a sense of the force I see.

# A Japanese Tale with A World-Wide Moral

Go back ten years, when computers in America are entering schools at a fast pace. Cross the Pacific to Japan at the peak of its domination of the international electronics industry. Look in a school. Nary a computer. Bizarre? Not if you know the structure of Japanese education. In America a school district, a school and even an individual teacher can decide to bring a computer into a classroom. In Japan the all-powerful ministry, the Mombasha, decides. But now it is paralyzed. I have had more than one glimpse by being invited as a consultant to its meetings. Talk, talk, talk. No different from education ministries I have visited in other countries. Education bureaucrats are specialists in conservatism and inaction.

Enter MITI. The famous Ministry of Industry has a very different way of doing business. These are the specialists in get-it-done. Now! Just-in-time thinking. The computer companies need new markets. The schools are there. Let's go.

Horrors! Panic at Mombasha. A powerful rival is entering its territory. Action needed. What to do?

HA! A marriage! For the first time ever, two of the usually proudly independent ministries undertake a joint program.

Very soon every school in Japan has computers far more powerful than those in American schools.

What makes English a learnable language for very young children is that—at least to some extent—it is so structured that simple parts can be learned in simple ways *and can be used as soon as they are learned.* I have been describing a process of learning the language of controlling computers like the way a baby learns to speak in English: In both cases the learner acquires fluency by doing simple things that get results—maybe simple results, but results all the same.

This is not like the kind of school learning in which you learn for many years before you can use what you have been learning for any purpose besides getting the teacher's approval. As we learn more we get more results. And as our need for more complex events grows, we learn what we need to learn. Children can learn to become fluent users of computers because so many segments of computer usage allow this kind of learning. Logo is designed to be one of them.

With this perspective I propose to leave Jason again and develop further the techniques of control by looking at a slightly different domain of work. I won't come back to Jason here but hope that you will try to do something like his project and use the techniques we are about to meet to carry it further.

# Making a Video Game

In the previous project you will no doubt have noticed that we were bordering on the edge of making a **video game**. Indeed, driving a turtle between obstacles could be the beginning of many different games. In this section I'll try to focus on what it might take to turn this into a particular well-known game—Pacman—choosing this because it is old enough to be familiar to many people.

First I want to emphasize the analogy between programming in MicroWorlds and using a physical construction set such as **Lego**. MicroWorlds is like Lego in supplying you with a collection of

# A Comparison of Power

Coming from an academic background, it took me some time to get used to the scale of operations and the raw power of media corporations.

I had been used to getting research funds from the Education Directorate of the National Science Foundation. The NSF has supported some pretty good, innovative education projects. No question about that. But compared with the thinking in media companies, its support is peanuts. A couple of million dollars is already a sizable project and $10 million is very exceptional. But a $10 million movie is called "low budget." Fifty million is not exceptional! Nobody ever gets to spend as much on making a new mathematics curriculum that could have national impact as a movie director can spend in six months on trying out his latest idea.

At least nobody did when education had to be publicly financed. Now the trend is very clear: The media industry is moving in and bringing, for better or for worse, its standards of appropriate scale.

Sometimes I look at the credits at the end of a movie and think what one could do if that number of talented people could work on a project of research to improve education!

Or think of another comparison of numbers of people. Nintendo in Seattle employs a staff of 150 people whose job is to answer questions that come from kids by mail or telephone. Just think of the reaction you'd get from the NSF or the Department of Education if you proposed paying 150 people to answer questions from kids about math. This is not enough to explain why kids handle Mario better than equations, but it's a start.

So that's my first force: the raw fire power of large corporations that are moving into active participation in education.

## The second force is the learning revolution.

Many people, including some very powerful ones, are coming to recognize a need for new approaches to learning. I give three kinds of evidence of the beginnings of this "learning revolution."

As I was writing these pages I learned that one more major corporation had decided to appoint a high-level executive to be manager of learning. Until quite recently this would have seemed a strange event. In the past decade there has been extensive discussion in business circles about restructuring corporations (or "re-engineering," to use the phrase that gained wide name recognition as the title of a best-selling book). Experience, however, has shown that attempts to reorganize a big corporation do not easily work: People go on doing things in the old way. Thus those in circles concerned with such issues have come to realize that *learning* is the key to change.

Learning in corporations might seem far removed from learning in schools. But talk about learning in corporate circles sends out waves that influence "what's in the air," and this in turn influences what kinds of decision might be made by a school board. Moreover, industry has money and has used some of it to sponsor innovations in schools. The chief executive officer of **IBM** has even written a book whose thesis is that School needs to be "reinvented," and that industry should take a leading role in making this possible.

Another perspective on the same issue: Once upon a time a young person would learn the work skills that would be used for the rest of life. That pattern worked when change was slow and people would be doing at the end of their lives something like what they learned to do at the beginning. It does not work in a world where most people are doing jobs that did not even exist when they were born. Maybe we are not quite in that world. But we are getting close enough to it to recognize a conundrum: If any skill a child learns will be out of date before it is used, then what on earth would you have a child learn? The answer is obvious: *The only competitive skill over the long haul is skill at learning.*

My third sign of a learning revolution is a phenomenal increase in the number of people who are learning all sorts of subjects from cooking to massage. It is a sign of the times that the Disney Corporation has created a place (the Disney Institute) designed for people who want to take a "learning vacation"—they are on vacation but are learning something.

So my second force for change in education is the growing momentum of a learning revolution—a shift in how people think about learning.

---

You can lead a kid to Euclid
but you can't make him think.

■

**The third force is the most powerful: child power.**
We are starting to see a shift of the driving force for change out of the schools and into the homes of people like you. Even if you do not personally do anything deliberately aimed at changing school, you are exerting a powerful influence on it by allowing your children to experience new, and in many ways much better, ways to learn. *Every child from a home that has a computer and a strong __learning culture__ is an agent for change in school.*

Becoming a change agent in their school (even if it is not consciously done) offers students great rewards and wonderful new opportunities for learning. But it also exposes them to some risk of getting themselves into trouble. Although you may not be able to prevent them from running the risk—or want to do so—being aware of it means you can give them the support they might need.

Listen to this story, which was told to me by a teacher, to see what I mean.

# A Teacher Learning Story

From the time the computers came I was afraid of the day my students would know more about programming than I ever will. At the beginning I had a big advantage. I came fresh from a summer workshop on **Logo** and the students were just beginning. But during the year they were catching up. They were spending more time on it than I could. Actually they didn't catch up the first year. But I knew that each year the children would know more because they would have had experience in previous grades, and because each year more of them would have computers at home. Besides, children are more in tune with computers than we grown-ups.

The first few times I noticed that the students had problems which I couldn't even understand, let alone solve. I struggled to avoid facing the fact that I could not keep up my stance of knowing more than they did. I tried to hide the fact. I was afraid that giving up this stance would undermine my authority as a teacher. But the situation became worse. Eventually I broke down and said "I don't understand your problem. Go discuss it with some of the others in the class who might be able to help." Which they did. Working together, the kids could figure out a solution.

Now the amazing thing is that what I was afraid of turned out to be a liberation. I no longer had to fear being exposed. It had already happened. I no longer had to pretend. And the wonderful thing was that I realized that my bluff was called for more than computers. I felt I could no longer pretend to know everything in other subjects as well. What a relief! It has changed my relationship with the children and with myself. My class has become much more of a collaborative community where we are all learning.

The students in this class were able to do more than get a teacher out of a pickle. They were responsible for changing that teacher's idea of teaching. No mean feat! The teacher might not have been sufficiently grateful but certainly was left with warm feelings. So all was well.

No, not quite. With another teacher, those kids might have been in big trouble. Some teachers cling longer to the facade of omniscience and resent students who allow their superior knowledge to be visible. As it was, the word might have gotten out in the school that these students had scored over the teacher and were to be treated as troublemakers.

Such reactions cannot be altogether circumvented. But they can be handled in better or worse ways. No doubt your kids are smart at handling school situations and could have handled this one. All the same, some support, wisdom and advice will help them, provided you can give these without stealing the ownership of what they are doing. At the least you can help them understand that in a conflict with the school on such issues you will be on their side. Perhaps you can help them develop a balanced way of thinking about risk-taking. Perhaps you can help develop their perspective on schools.

Our learning story illustrates the positive way that kids can change the learning culture of the school. There is also a negative way. It may be more potent in the end and even more dangerous. But it is what will prevail if school does not change its ways.

It seems clear to me that children believe in school less and less. This is why disciplinary problems are increasing. School is becoming delegitimized in the eyes of children as they come to see how far it lags behind the society it is supposed to serve, and as they come to understand how backward the ways of learning are that it continues to espouse.

*Do we really expect children to sit still for the predigested curriculum of the elementary school when they have known the freedom to explore knowledge on the information highways of the world, and when they have been used to planning complex projects and finding for themselves the knowledge and advice they need to conduct them?*

# How Can A Parent Influence School?

I propose a five-point program:

### Point 1: Understand the forces of resistance to change.

First it is essential to understand the dynamics of change and resistance to change in schools. Let's look more closely at the pendulum swing of school technology mentioned earlier, starting from the romantic period of microcomputers around 1980.

A LEARNING STORY

## A Learning Story about How School Learns

Up to the mid-eighties there were few microcomputers in schools, but those few were almost all in the classrooms of visionary teachers who encouraged usage in a "progressive" spirit, cutting across School's practices of balkanized curriculum and impersonal rote learning. By the mid-eighties the movement was changing direction sharply. The driving force and the power were moving from teachers to school administrations—most often at the city or even at the state level.

When there were few computers in the school the administration was content to leave them in the classrooms of teachers who showed greatest enthusiasm, and these were generally teachers who were excited about the computer as an instrument of change. But as the numbers grew and computers became something of a status symbol for a school, the administration moved into the act. From an administrator's point of view it made more sense to put the computers together in one room—often misleadingly named a "computer lab."

In the worst cases the computer lab becomes a place for drill and practice in the traditional school materials. Most often the school buys what is known as an ILS (Integrated Learning System), which makes no demands on anyone to do anything new. The teacher merely supervises. The students do what the computer tells them.

In better cases the computer lab is placed under the control of a specialized computer teacher. By an inexorable logic the next step is to introduce a curriculum for the computer.

But in both cases the subversive features of the computer are eroded away: Instead of cutting across and so challenging the very idea of subject boundaries, the computer now defines a new subject; instead of moving the initiative from impersonal curriculum to the excited live exploration by a student, the computer is now used to reinforce hierarchical thinking. What started as a subversive instrument of change is neutralized by the system and converted into an instrument of consolidation.

---

The shift from a radically subversive instrument in the classroom to a blunted conservative instrument in the computer lab comes neither from a lack of knowledge nor from a lack of software. I explain it by an innate intelligence of School, which acts like any living organism in defending itself against a foreign body. It puts into motion an immune reaction whose end result is to digest and assimilate the intruder. Progressive teachers know very well how to use the computer for their own ends as an instrument of change; School knows very well how to nip this subversion in the bud. No one in the story acts out of ignorance about computers, although they might be naive in failing to understand the sociological drama in which they are actors.

Fortunately this story needs one qualification. Nothing ever works perfectly, and although the logic of the computer lab's development is retrograde compared with visionary teachers in their own classrooms, often the computer teacher is one of those visionaries at heart and finds ways to some very remarkable work with the students in the lab. I have known many who fought the restrictions imposed by time (seeing students for an hour or two a week) and curriculum by organizing an after-school club or even a special voluntary daily class an hour before school officially opened.

## Point 2: Find allies; strategize.

The major moral of the previous story is that there will be differences within the school between teachers who would like nothing better than to do exciting work with computers and administrations who do not necessarily have deep reasons to oppose these teachers but find it easier to do so.

If you are going to be effective in influencing the school you have to find the place where you can put a spark to the right flammable material. Identify the issues in which there may be conflicts where you can swing the balance; find out the people who have problems you can help solve. You have to be seen by at least some people in the school as a resource willing to help. It is not bad if some see you as a troublemaker, but it is very bad if everyone does.

## Point 3: Support teacher development.

Consider a choice between two approaches to using computers in which there is a trade-off between how much teacher learning is needed and how much benefit is gained by the students. Method A makes modest promises, but these come immediately and at little cost. An inexpensive piece of software and two hours of "teacher training" are all that are needed. Method B is more ambitious in what it promises in the long run but will only get there when teachers have advanced along a learning curve that might take several years before students are really gaining. It also costs more.

The trend in most schools today is strongly in favor of A. Examples of this trend are favoring computer literacy curriculum over striving for **technological fluency**. It is cheaper and easier to give students a superficial knowledge of six superficial pieces of software than to delve deeply into the uses of any one. A severe case of penny-wise, pound-foolish!

# Success

In 1986 Oskar Arias, who later won the Nobel Peace Prize for bringing an end to hostilities in Central America, was running for president in Costa Rica on a platform that included bringing computer technology into the schools of his country. After he won the election he initiated a process to decide how to do this. The discussion soon polarized into two camps.

One party argued that the mode of use should be as easy on the teacher as possible. Many of the teachers in the rural districts had very little experience with technology and no formal education in anything technical. These teachers, it was argued, would be excluded by computer uses that required technical skills. Thus this party argued for using drill-and-practice software; had this side won, the contract would probably have gone to a company offering the kind of ("teacher-proof") turnkey system in which the computer is switched on and goes.

The other party did not quite put their argument in the following words, but as things worked out it could have been stated as: On the contrary, make it as hard as possible for the teachers.

The debate was settled by an experiment in which a group of teachers participated in an intensive three-week **Logo** workshop. Although there is no objective way to make such measurements, I think it was obvious to all observers that an exceptional quantity of learning took place in these weeks. And I think it is almost as obvious that this happened because the participating teachers felt that much more was involved than a technical improvement in learning basic skills. These teachers were making a personal assertion of their will to appropriate this modern thing, they were making a professional assertion against a view of teaching as a lowly profession and they were making a national assertion against the view of their country as underdeveloped. Many of them were also making an assertion of gender: A large percentage of elementary school teachers are women, and the organizers of the project had the good sense to reflect this in the selection process.

The outcome was an exemplary program in which hundreds of teachers, most of whom indeed had no technical background, learned to program in Logo and derived a great new sense of confidence in themselves and their country by mastering something that was experienced as challenging, modern, difficult and "not for people like them." This is in quite remarkable contrast with the position adopted by many American school districts that Logo is "educationally good" but "too hard for teachers"!

# A Piece of Symbolic Advice:
# "No" to "Teacher Training"

In the context of education, the word "training" carries meanings derogatory to the intellectual value of teachers. If one asks them "Is the goal of teacher training to train teachers to train children?" the answer will usually be a stunned silence or a strong negative. No one wants to use the word training to describe what children are supposed to get out of school. When we talk about children we use words more respectful of intellectual growth such as "education" or "development" or "socialization." Why the asymmetry? The answer is clear enough: Because School has a powerful tendency to see teachers as technicians doing a technical job, and for this the word training is perfectly appropriate.

■

## Point 4: Support fluency over literacy.

In particular support uses of the computer in which the student really uses the computer rather than learning about it, and especially those in which the student uses it in a personally empowered way by carrying out projects that give a genuine sense of competence.

## Point 5: Support or lobby for the establishment of teacher-controlled alternative schools or programs.

One of the sources of resistance to change in schools is a consequence of the size and diversity of the stake holders. Any significant change must seem legitimate in the eyes of the administration, the teachers and, though their influence is less, the parents, as well as more distant stake holders—superintendents, school-board members, town or city officials and even the local media, all of whom have to be taken into account. The result is that the only changes that ever get decided (and are not subsequently sabotaged) are minimal common denominators of many varied beliefs.

Serious innovations need some degree of voluntary assent by like-minded people. In some school systems (I have seen this work best in New York City) a group of teachers can propose to create a program based on an approach to teaching and even on choice of content very different from the general practice of that school system. They have to convince the school board that the program is serious and that a sufficient number of parents will want to enroll their children in it. The criteria for getting approval might be tough. But they do not include conformity.

The movement towards charter schools follows the same direction of allowing a like-minded set of people to get together to decide on an approach to education. Although there are some examples of an entire established school making a change in policy, attempts at radical change more often run into high resistance. The only generally effective strategy for change is to get together people who are already converted and find a way for them to develop their ideas.

It is quite remarkable that in this country that vaunts the idea of entrepreneurship and initiative in the economy, it has taken so long to accept such ideas in education. But there is no room for doubt that such a trend is at last getting under way, and that parents who have seen powerful modes of learning actually working in their homes are in the best position to strengthen and direct it. One early manifestation of this trend in America is the home-schooling movement.

# The Homeschooling Option

Not send your children to school? For most people this seems unthinkable, not only because of the practical problems of managing life with the kids at home, all day every day, but especially because it defies one of our most solidly established social customs. Children of school-going age are almost defined by their relationship to school. One of the first questions an adult will ask after encountering a child is, "What grade are you in?" Looking for analogous situations, I found myself thinking that attitudes about children not going to school are not unlike the attitudes people used to have, for example when I was a teenager some fifty years ago, about cohabiting couples not being married.

Although it is hard to find accurate figures, it is widely believed that the families of about one percent of American children of school-going age are doing what they call homeschooling. These families do not all choose this for the same reason. Some parents keep their children out of school for religious reasons. Many keep young children at home because they enjoy them so much. But the fastest-growing segment of homeschoolers are choosing this option for a reason that is closest to the issues I have been discussing in this book: dissatisfaction with the **learning culture** found in schools.

Even when there is a choice between schools, it is often reminiscent of Henry Ford's statement about the early Model T: "You can have any color you like as long as it's black." In many cases parents make their decision for homeschooling only after putting great energy into finding a satisfactory school and doing everything they can to improve the schools they do find.

Some cybertopians believe that the presence of computers will cause the quality as well as the quantity of homeschooling to develop very quickly, to go very far and to be all together for the good. For example, the title of Lewis Perelman's book—*School's Out*—expresses the idea as forcefully as the book argues approvingly that educational software has already made school obsolete.

I am sure that in the next few years the number of families opting for homeschooling will increase as the presence of computers diminishes many of the obstacles to homeschooling and increases many of its advantages. But in the longer run I would predict a more complex process in which, rather than a victory of one option over the other, we'll see significant changes in both school and homeschooling. The form I would most like to see this take is a blurring of the boundaries between them. One way in which this might happen in a not-very-distant future (though still not tomorrow or next year) is that the two movements of change might meet halfway: The development of small alternative schools away from the traditional framework might meet the development of cooperative arrangements set up by homeschooling families to share the work of tending their children. The important immediate step I would encourage families on both sides to take is establishing more contact for sharing ideas and experiences. This could benefit both sides.

Few parents of school-going children think of the homeschooling movement as a source of ideas that could be helpful to them. It seems far too exotic and removed from their concerns. But many of the problems faced by people trying to improve their home learning environment are the same, whether their intention is to replace school or to supplement it. In fact much of the best discussion of educational issues I have found on the Internet is in Web sites run by homeschoolers.

On reflection this is not really surprising. Parents who have decided to keep their children out of school are under greater pressure than most to think up and share learning-rich activities, most of which can be adapted to the needs and possibilities of schoolgoing children. Another source of pressure on homeschooling parents to think about learning comes from having to take personal responsibility for problems usually left to professionals. For example, I ran into a lively and very well-informed discussion by homeschoolers about the idea of learning disabilities. The discussion included stories by parents who had decided for homeschooling when school psychologists applied labels such as "learning disabled" to children who showed great learning ability at home. In some cases the problems that drew the attention of the psychologists continued in the homeschooling environment; in many cases the "disability" quickly evaporated.

Another rich source of ideas in the homeschooling community is the contribution of children who take far more responsibility for their own learning than one sees in the average school or family setting. On some Web sites I encountered thoughtful writing by children about their learning experiences and a desire to share these with other people. In reading them I was struck once again by how wrong critics are when they contrast the so-called socializing virtues of school with the so-called isolating tendencies of computers. These children were using computers as a means to enter—in fact to create—something more authentic as a *learning community* than can be found in most schools.

Sharing ideas between homeschooling families and those who have a strong interest in building home learning cultures without taking the extreme step of abandoning the school system is the obvious advantage of using computers. But I also see two other, possibly less obvious, advantages.

One of these is specifically related to computer usage. I would not have been able to find Web sites run by homeschoolers if none of these families owned and used computers. But what I saw in them showed me that their uses of computers were not always the most sophisticated; exchanges with people who have more developed computer cultures would help them make better use of their own computers.

The other specific advantage is more political, and a small step towards the meeting of movements of educational change from inside *and* outside the school system. Even in the short run there is room for a more porous separation between those who are "in school" and those who are "out of school." For example, some communities allow homeschoolers to participate in some school activities so that they can be partially in and partially out. I believe that this kind of arrangement is in everyone's interest, and so a good topic around which to build an alliance of parents—schoolers or homeschoolers—who want to be active in the advancement of learning.

An idea for a more elaborated form of porous separation on which I have been working myself is the creation of high-tech *community learning centers* designed to be used both by schools and by other members of the community, including adults as well as children who may be schoolers, homeschoolers or school dropouts. In a model on which I have collaborated with Chuck Tetro, a leader in job training and career development, such community learning centers allow schools the opportunity to gain experience with **technological fluency** without making a full commitment in advance and also allow people, including youngsters who might have gained technological fluency at home, to further their own development and perform a valuable community service by participating in the growth of a computer learning culture in a public place.

In the long run, the development of learning places outside of schools—that may or may not be porously connected with schools

and that may or may not combine learning with community service or even remunerative work—is a possible route into a learning environment of the future in which school in anything like its
traditional form might be considered just one of many equally
valued, publicly supported places of learning. With many such
choices, the concept of homeschooling will have merged into the
concept of a learning society.

# Future

In previous chapters I avoided examples using stuff you couldn't buy today. But hoping that a peep at where we are going will show the meaning of where we are, I end with three speculative stories about children and technology, each running from the distant past into the very near future.

## Building Toys

I assume that as long as our species existed, and perhaps even longer, children have spent time building structures out of natural materials such as sticks, stones, mud and sand. It would be fascinating to know what they built in times gone by. Could children have been engaged in similar activities across all those millennia? Since today's children will tell you they are building relatively modern objects—a house, a castle or a tower—it is clear that details must have changed. But it is not entirely implausible that children in the distant past would have built very similar structures and described them differently. The idea of building a tower as high as possible does not need the inspiration of a skyscraper or a biblical story. The activity is suggested by the material, and one might even guess that what children have always been able to do inspired adult feats that could not be realized until the technology was ready.

Little as we know about the ancient history of children's building, we have even less scientifically established knowledge about its specific contribution to intellectual development. However, when one looks carefully at children at work on their construction projects, it seems obvious that they are practicing and presumably developing skills that are far more complex than many of those that software intended for small children purports to teach them. One best-selling software seems to be trying to teach four- or five-year-old children "the concept of big and small" by asking them to match small and big items of clothing with small and big figures of people. Frankly I think this is "baby stuff" compared with what children of that age are actually teaching themselves. I invite you to form your own opinion by building a tower out of whatever materials you have at hand—sugar cubes are excellent if you happen to use them in your family.

Activities like building a tower obviously contribute to developing an intuitive sense of physics concepts such as balance and stability. But very much more is involved. Focus on the observation and concentration you need in increasing degrees as the tower grows higher. Focus on how the task might be exercising and perhaps honing your idea of symmetry. Think about how many metaphors from building physical structures we use in talking about mental activities: "Each argument supported the next but in the end it all collapsed like a house of cards."

Building a sand castle on the beach mobilizes very different kinds of thinking. The tower is best made working alone or with one collaborator; for the sand castle the more the better, as long as there is enough social cohesion of purpose. The tower depended on minute adjustments; here it is the natural flow of the material that must be respected in guiding big movements.

In both cases there is a sense of satisfaction as persistence in the face of setbacks is rewarded by the translation of a fantasy into reality. We could go on for a long time, but these few comments are enough to establish (as if there could have been any doubt!) that childish building touches cognitively rich layers of experience. So I'll move on with my sketch of the evolution of children's building.

Up to the last few centuries, fabricated building materials for children were rare luxuries, but with the Industrial Revolution came a profusion of building blocks of wood and later more complex metal components, such as Meccano and Erector sets. With the arrival of plastics came a bifurcation. One branch of development continued the normal incremental improvement of what was being made before. Plastic blocks could be made more colorful, more decorated and less expensive than those made of wood. The other branch of development was more than a mere shift of material. The story of how it happened is worth telling, especially since it is a beautiful example of serendipitous discovery that should be known to the millions of children who daily use its fruits.

The story starts in the 1930s, in the days of the Great Depression. A Danish carpenter called Christiansen, unable to get work on new houses, began a little business of his own making wooden toy trucks. He found that he liked this so much better that even when conditions improved and he could have gone back to his old work he preferred to stay with toymaking. The war came and went, and Christiansen was still making wooden trucks. His business grew a little but was still just a few people making low-tech toys.

But new technologies were developing. Among them the technology of plastics, and this led to the idea of improving the toy by adding a load of plastic bricks. This was done and indeed proved to be a success. But not anything like the kind of success that came from the idea that in retrospect, like all great ideas, seems obvious. If the bricks could only stick together they would be a wonderful construction set. AHA! The idea of **Lego** was born. (And if you wonder why it is so called, it is an internationalization of a Danish phrase that means "let's play.")

Today there are little Lego bricks in ninety percent of homes with children in the U.S. and Europe! Its popularity reflects its quality as a building material. In comparison with wooden blocks it has enormously greater range. In comparison with more versatile metal sets like Meccano and Erector, it still wins for the range of what can be built, but it has an even greater advantage in a quality that makes it an excellent material for the **Bricoleur** as well as the Planner.

Watch a child improvise with Lego. The finished product need not have been planned in advance or, even if it has, the idea can change fluidly as the construction proceeds. The entire process has something in common with shaping clay. It shares the "morphing" quality so dear to children. I see this quality as drawing children into more complex levels of activity and developing a creative intellectual style that favors flow and openness—and in many cases in which flow is not necessarily essential, the quality still allows more intimate involvement with the activity.

These special qualities led me in the mid-eighties to begin a collaboration with the makers of Lego, who provided funding (and more intellectual forms of support) for a research laboratory known as the **Lego/Logo Lab** within the M.I.T. Media Laboratory. Over the course of ten years many researchers have brought diverse skills and perspectives to their work there on what we see as the birth of a new stage in the development of children's construction materials. The spirit of what is emerging from this is illustrated by the following fantasy scenario. The scenario includes ideas that have been brought by M.I.T. professor Mitchel Resnick, who has a background in physics and in journalism; Steve Ocko, a gifted inventor of toys; Edith Ackermann, a former student of **Jean Piaget**; Fred Martin, who came from a background in mechanical engineering and has learned to be a master teacher of teachers; and Rick Borovoy, who represents a new generation of graduate students.

In our fantasy scenario, children are constructing what looks like a robotic creature from a science-fiction movie. It has six spindly legs, somewhat like a spider's, and walks in a wobbly sort of way. Four-year-old Ann is giving it a head with what she calls a "talking mouth," and indeed as soon as the mouth is attached the creature begins to babble. After momentary pleasure at this effect she decides she doesn't really like the way it "talks" and begins to hunt around in the piles of pieces scattered all over the floor. Eventually she announces to Tom, "I found a speech brain." As soon as the tiny piece is attached, the creature's steady stream of babble is replaced by a more orderly flow of recognizable words. Tom says "I'll make mine so it will hear if yours makes a calling sound and go to it."

It may seem fanciful to imagine children engaged in making things that not long ago could only be encountered in advanced laboratories of "artificial intelligence" or "artificial life." It is not at all fanciful.

In a school in Rhode Island, Fred Martin is working with teachers on developing projects in which junior high school students build models incorporating a small computer that they program to give the model interesting behaviors. For example the model might be a robot that finds its way around obstacles or goes to a light.

Of course this is still far short of my fantasy. The computers used by these students are small enough to be built into a Lego model, but they still have a long way to go to fit my scenario, in which they are small enough not to be a noticeable presence in the model. On the functional side, the computers are simple enough for elementary school students to use in original projects, but my fantasy requires their use to be accessible—and desirable—to four-year-old children. And although Lego pieces allow a lot of flexibility for building, the spider robot will require a richer set of materials. But within a few years all these elements will be there in laboratory prototypes that could be mass produced at affordable prices. After that, how long it takes for the fantasy to get into playrooms will depend on people in suits making business decisions. But with the prospect of pioneering a whole new market for toys of the future, it is unlikely that none of the "suits" will have the imagination to go after it. *Watch for such products!*

The fantasy of a small Lego piece playing the role of a "talking mouth" is even further from getting into the toy stores, but objects of this nature are real enough to form the subject of a Media Lab doctoral thesis by Rick Borovoy, working under the direction of Mitchel Resnick. If you are a new parent, your kids will probably miss this phase, but your grandchildren won't!

Naturally you will ask: What will children get from this "build-an-animal" kit? Just as I did in the discussion of building a tower, I could begin by noting knowledge belonging to specific domains, such as physics. But I attach more importance to general cognitive attitudes and skills. Perhaps the most important of these is continuing the early childhood habit of asking "How does that work?" and having a fair chance of finding an answer. I have already expressed my concern at how the growing opacity of contemporary technology undermines this habit. Not only are the workings of many of the more intriguing objects of the modern world made physically invisible by their fabrication, they are also made conceptually **opaque** by the exclusion from school and culture of the principles on which they function. How do the automatic controls of household devices know what to do? How does an airplane's auto pilot "know" where to go? How does a guided missile reach its target? To say that these machines are "programmed" to do such things invests the idea of programming with mystery. Giving the child the opportunity to build models that will perform similar functions demystifies. It makes automatic objects at least conceptually **transparent**.

I mention two other kinds of reasons for believing that a build-an-animal kit would be great for children.

One is that this kind of work evokes the emotional force of the love affair with computers and marries it with the acquisition and use of a wide range of valuable knowledge, including knowledge about our bodies. The models use the same kinds of mechanisms as our bodies do so valuably in maintaining their temperature despite variations in the atmosphere, and so frustratingly in maintaining their weight despite sometimes desperate variations in diet. Building these "cybernetic" or "robotic" animals leads to a deeper and more personal understanding of physiological as well as physical and psychological principles.

My other reason for liking the idea of children using computers as components of a construction kit is that it breaks away from the idea that the computer is something separate from the real world of physical things. What the children make might be guided by fantasy (which is surely good) but cannot be described as a virtual reality (a concept that raises far more complex issues about when it is good and when it is bad for children).

# Social Toys: "Little People" Made of Bits

Think of children arranging dolls in a family group, cuddling teddy bears, lining up tin soldiers or pushing cars along roads marked on the sand. This is a modern form of another children's activity that must have existed for millennia.

Here too the historical pattern consists of tens of thousands of years with very little change, a few centuries of moderate change and a modern explosion of novelty in the wake of new technologies and new materials. I complained that psychologists have given insufficient attention to understanding how and what construction kits contribute to learning. In the case of social toys, however, a huge amount of scientific and scholarly work has been applied to confirm what any parent can see: Playing with them obviously exercises, and seems to contribute to, the growth of social and relational skills. Few parents, teachers or psychologists would question the value of this kind of fantasy play. So as computation increasingly pervades the world of children, our concern must be to ensure that what is good about play is at least preserved (and hopefully enhanced) as the concept of "toy" inevitably changes.

Social toys will develop in many directions. In fact the construction kits of the previous section can be seen as one of these, for what I called a build-an-animal kit could have a "build-a-doll" kit as a close relative. Here, however, I shall focus on just one direction, one which could be called the development of digital dolls: entities that are like dolls but that exist only as bits in a computer (or, if you like to split hairs, as pixels on the computer screen).

*My Make Believe Castle* is an early, still-primitive example of this genre of software. A prince on the screen can be placed on a horse and set to riding around the castle. A witch can be made to walk back and forth, cackling maliciously every time she passes the princess. These are toys. They differ from traditional dolls and stuffed animals and lead soldiers in the stuff out of which they are made. They are not made of tangible matter made of atoms; they are made of a new kind of stuff made of bits. But they are toys nonetheless because they serve many of the functions of toys.

Of course there are differences between material toys made of atoms and computational toys made of bits. In some ways the digitals are clearly inferior—so far there is no way to cuddle them. But the comparison of how well they serve the function of toys is by no means one-sided. Each has advantages and each has limitations. While you can't cuddle with a teddy bear on the screen and you don't have the physical feeling of pushing the car, the screen toy does more by itself. It has more built-in personality and gives you more surprises.

These qualities of digital toys, however, can be seen from opposite perspectives. For example, the "real," cuddly teddy bear of atoms might have less built-in personality than a screen bear that talks and generally does more, but this deficiency becomes a strength for a child who takes advantage of creating a personality for the old-fashioned teddy. The challenge for parents is to keep an eye on the balance. I often hear people who make cursory judgments too quickly. They don't realize to what extent the digital toy can have the fantasy and social aspects of traditional dolls, but they also fail to pay attention to the shallowness of characters in many CD-ROM productions intended for children. Nicky the dragon in *My Make Believe Castle* is an example of a digital toy with enough built-in personality to start a good relationship and enough openness to allow a child to project much more. On the other hand, the "master of ceremonies" or "mentor" characters in a lot of teaching software often set up a shallow model of cuteness as the dominant character trait.

Looking a little way into the future, I see a burgeoning of roles for digital toys and a division on the issue of how much built-in personality they will have. First, I envisage toys that have more personality—more subtle and more complex—than those we see today. Second, I envisage the possibility that these more subtle and complex personalities will not all be given at the factory but will develop later. Perhaps the toy's owner will program it or perhaps do something more akin to "training" or even "educating" than to programming or perhaps the development will be more autonomous. Third, I imagine that digital toys will be transportable to many different digital worlds.

Perhaps the third of these is most in need of clarification. In present-day software, characters can sometimes be changed but can only very, very exceptionally be moved from one "application" to another. For example, suppose a child likes the character Nicky in

*My Make Believe Castle* and wants to take him into another software—or perhaps wants to make a new software production in which Nicky can be incorporated. The technical means for this are rapidly developing independently of any interest in children.

I first heard from **Alan Kay** the idea of developing a tool kit with which a child could construct a digital fish and place it in a digital aquarium to see how well it managed in cooperation and in competition with fish made by other people. Designing such digital creatures would bring children into contact with ideas from many fields of science. It would help them make sense of biology, as Jenny's computer experience helped her make sense of grammar. It would make topics like evolution far more concrete, allowing students to understand the difficulties faced by current theories as well as their strengths. It would introduce children to some other modern fields that go by such names as ecology, ethology, systems theory and cybernetics. And it would be a superb way to develop **computer fluency** as well as pick up elementary forms of ideas from computer science.

I would not expect designing digital fish to diminish interest in real fish. Quite the contrary, the digital aquarium would make real fish more interesting by making them more intellectually **transparent**—what lies behind the behavior patterns of real fish would be more visible and so more intriguing (and instructive) to a child who has struggled to give similar behaviors to a digital fish.

It is interesting to speculate that as digital toys come to have more complex behaviors and personalities and become capable of following their owners to different sites, they become more like pets than like dolls—a good example of the computer's tendency to blur distinctions that once seemed absolutely clear-cut.

This idea of "net pets" joins several lines of current research. Some involve children directly: Amy Bruckman, a student at the Media Lab, has probed the idea of giving children the tools to program digital pets (and other objects) in a kind of cyberplace called a MUD (or multi-user dungeon, because of its descent from the game *Dungeons and Dragons*). A related line of research that is being pursued for applications in the business world is the development of "autonomous agents" endowed with enough "intelligence" to do a job such as filtering your email (like a watchdog) or setting out to visit sites on the Net for you. In this spirit I imagine a child sending a pet-agent to visit Grandma as a step beyond birthday cards.

While these ideas are still at the laboratory stage of development, you can get a feel for the construction of digital worlds from the popular products of the company Maxis and by using search engines to find the latest reports of research on agents.

# Reading, 'Riting and 'Rithmetic

I have kept to the end my most controversial belief, which is that the time has come to examine deeply our society's commitment to the "three R's" as almost synonymous with early education. Most people—parents or teachers—will insist that the R's are just one component of School's balanced intellectual diet, together with understanding history and science and developing creativity, social skills and moral principles. Yet despite these protestations, the overwhelming importance given to the R's is shown by the widespread tendency to judge schools according to how many children are "reading at grade level" and by the enormous anxiety evoked when an individual child does not read at the time that has been decreed for this to happen.

The identification of "reading" with "education" is also seen in the use of "literacy rate" as a measure of how well countries are "developing," and in the periodic yells of panic when the press trots out a figure showing how many Americans have been shown by some test to be "functionally illiterate."

What I want to call in question is not the indisputable value in the present-day world of being able to read, write and calculate. What is disputable is whether the priority we give to the R's will continue to make sense as other media for access to knowledge become available. I not only believe that the priority should shift, but that it inevitably will do so. I also believe that although this shift will take time to happen, it has such profound implications for thinking about school, and indeed about the nature of childhood, that it urgently deserves attention now.

Before elaborating my reasons for believing this I must make two qualifications.

First, I do not believe that the shift would mean that children will no longer learn to read. In fact, somewhat paradoxically, I believe that taking off the pressure will result in more children learning to read at earlier ages and with less stress. For there is no doubt in my mind that the anxiety shown by adults when children do not read, and the enormous pressure placed on them to do so, are major causes of so-called reading disabilities.

Second, I indignantly reject the suggestion often made by advocates of "back to basics" that they have a monopoly on tough educational methods. There has recently been an epidemic of books and articles on the theme that children are not learning because School attaches more importance to "making them feel good" than to having them learn the basics. These critics of School are right in their perception that many schools practice indulgent policies based on the idea that learning should be "easy." In Chapter 3 I took my own dig at this idea, which has been largely taken up by the culture of children's software. But there are many ways to achieve high standards and to nurture the taste for difficult work. In fact I would not even count the drill-and-practice approach to "the basics" among them. Far from developing habits of hard intellectual work, it gets results on test scores (when it works at all) by developing a tolerance for mindless regimentation.

This said, I invite you to go back to the story about Ian and the videotape with which I opened my book.

We met Ian at the beginning of an epistemological transition: a major change in his relationship with knowledge which is best understood in terms of a three-stage model of kinds of learning or relationships with knowledge.

The first stage in this model is characterized by the self-directed, experiential, nonverbal **home-style learning** that is dominant in the first two or three years of a child's life. The second stage is less pure. It creeps up gradually as more and more learning takes the form that will culminate in **school-style learning**. This is learning that is dependent on the willingness of adults to explain or teach. It is largely verbal. It reaches its purest form in school, where the child gives up control of the learning process to the curriculum and the lesson plans of a teacher.

Reading enters in two ways as a central concern of this second stage. On the one hand, reading and writing are essential to the functioning of stage-two teaching. The teacher cannot deliver all knowledge in lecture style and cannot expect students to remember everything without taking notes or referring to textbooks. But at the same time, learning to read provides what will for some students be an escape into the third stage.

In essential ways the third stage is a return to the first: The pursuit of knowledge is once more under the learner's control. Of course this pursuit may draw on other people and even be conducted collectively. But the essential feature is that the individual has the means to seek knowledge and sources of knowledge, such as voluntary association with others.

Not everyone reaches the third stage. It is seen in all those adults who eventually gain the ability to pursue knowledge independently through the use of books and libraries and other instruments of research. Scientists or historians following careers in pursuit of new knowledge are clearly in this stage, as are creative businesspeople, journalists and physicians. I assume that readers of this book are there. But the essence of stage three is not a matter of having college degrees or any other stamp of institutional approval. A school dropout who keeps abreast of what is happening in the world and tries to use this knowledge creatively may be more advanced in stage-three learning than many graduates. Indeed I know cases of students who dropped out of school *because* their powerful, precocious development of stage-three learning made school's regimentation intolerable. Nevertheless, most kids who drop out of school do so because they have lost the spontaneous desire to learn that they had as young children. Many of these are victims of the dependency characteristic of stage two.

Nor is stage three synonymous with "literacy." The whole point of this discussion is that new media are opening new routes of access other than the ability to read to that kind of relationship with knowledge. Indeed, stage three must have existed before writing, and even in our writing-dominated world individuals find other routes to intellectual creativity. I know an intellectually creative young man, certainly a person of stage three, who is functionally dyslexic to the extent that it takes him an hour to decipher (rather than "read") a printed page, but who successfully found his way through high school without revealing his disability. Among his many "tricks" was developing such skills of social charm and such powers of deduction from scraps of knowledge that he could substitute lunches with his classmates for library research as a means of getting the information he needed to do school assignments. He even plausibly attributes to these practices a fine honing of deductive skills that has served him well as an adult. The skill of putting together the whole picture from scraps of lunch-table conversation constitutes a large part of what is required to be a good doctor, journalist, scientist, businessman, parent, spouse or friend.

Thinking about this young man who could not read provides a valuable window of insight into what new media can offer children. Would life as a high school student have been very different for him if he had had access to the technologies that have been developed in the fifteen or so years since he was there? Obviously someone in his position today would have a better chance of being able to get at information in digital form. There is much more of it, and digital media offer better search procedures to locate whatever exists. Admittedly most procedures involve using text, but his difficulty was less in recognizing the isolated word than in making sense of sentences and whole pages of text.

Thinking about the kid who can't read isolated words because he has not yet learned (rather than because he is dyslexic) allows me to introduce a fundamental shift in thinking about how children might learn to read, as well as about how they might get along without it: *Bypassing reading may help children learn to read.*

How that can be is seen by looking more carefully at the statement that Ian could not read. He could not read a newspaper or even a story. But he did know how to recognize the tape he wanted. I didn't think at the time to investigate how he did this but since then have learned from better observers that what I suspected was probably true: Children who "can't read" can sometimes recognize patterns of words sufficiently well enough to choose a tape, just as they can recognize their own names on a letter or especially on a package that therefore probably contains a gift from a grandparent or aunt who lives far away. My observation about grandson Sam, whose first "writing" was naming his KidPix products, is closely related.

The deeper point I see in all this is that the traditional learning environment of a baby is a good one for spoken words but not for written words, and that in the new learning environment this is changing. The life of a baby allows even isolated approximations to a single spoken word to serve such important purposes as expressing needs and feelings. It provides rich opportunities for observing and imitating the act of speaking. But until now the written language in little approximate, isolated pieces has been essentially useless to a child. Yet Sam had watched adults use the keyboard in ways that served his purposes and that he wanted to imitate. And to do so he did not have to pass a high threshold of being able to read a story. He did not even have to spell "correctly"— his invented spellings did just as well.

The presence of digital media bypasses the alphabet as the medium for stories and information but opens a new function for alphabetic skills used as a *means of control*. Typing makes things happen. So does reading: Recognizing words on a screen can be a step in an interactive search. It can be used to control a process that will lead to a desired end—maybe entering a Web site, maybe finding the video story one wants. And if you get it wrong something happens all the same, and you either take advantage of it or try again, just as you did when you were first learning to speak. These, I think, are ideal conditions for learning.

Thus in summary and in conclusion I invite you to think about a new route into reading and a new function for it in the life of a developing child. I am not asking you to think about these things because I am predicting they will be the way of the future, though I strongly suspect that some things like them will be important developments. I am asking you to think about them in the spirit of breaking with the **ostrich**-like assumption that things will happen the way they happened in the past.

# Conclusion

Writing a concluding piece for a book was once a rather definitive act that might be experienced with trauma or with relief, depending on one's personality and how one felt about the work. Today as I sit down to do it, I hear in my head the classic advice to a graduation speaker to explain that the word "commencement" is really apt because the event is not the end of a phase of life but a beginning of the next. This is not *adieu* but *au revoir . . . do svidanya . . . till we meet again* in cyberspace. For if there has been any communication between us at all, that should happen. And if there hasn't, I don't expect you would be reading this anyway.

This new modern relationship between reader and author takes the burden away from writing an end piece. For I can write a new one every day and post it up on the Web page that I have already promised to maintain!

So taking the "new beginning" idea literally, I am going to end as I might have liked to begin if I could have assumed that we had enough common understanding of words, ideas and examples, and if I had already gone through the experience of writing the rest of the book.

Of course I could simply have called this a recapitulation and skipped all this explanation. But I like the feeling of belonging to the cyberage.

Children are in love with computers. Some parents are worried and have good reason to be. Some are worried needlessly. Some are not worried about issues that ought to be worrying them:

## WORRY:

Many parents fear that the computer will suck their kids into a virtual world where nothing is real. This fear takes different forms. Those who are inclined to think metaphysically are afraid that children will grow up with a false sense of reality. Perhaps they will not know the difference between the real and the simulated. Perhaps they will know the difference but prefer the simulated. They will become superficial thinkers lacking in concern for deep philosophical or religious or spiritual issues.

Parents who think more practically fear that children will be gullible and easily duped if they become used to taking the world not simply at face value but, worse yet, at *interface value*. . . .

## ANSWER:

Yes it can happen. But it need not.

The equation computer = virtual is not necessarily true. Sometimes it is itself a mark of a superficial view of things. Are the words on my computer screen real or simulated? If we confuse words with ink, these words are superficial, simulated words. But if we look deeper to see what really matters about words, they are as real as any written with quill and ink.

The same point is true about many of the activities discussed in *The Connected Family*. When a child uses the computer as a material for creation, what is made is just as real as if it were made out of wood and (if you want to split this hair) more real than, say, a dance danced or a poem spoken.

As for being gullible: Writing computer programs is a great training in hard-nosed suspicion of the way things seem to be.

WORRY:

They'll grow up believing that everything the computer says is true.

ANSWER:

Not quite the same point so I'll give it not quite the same answer: Not if they are experienced in programming they won't—they'll be in more danger of never believing *anything* a computer says.

WORRY:

The computer encourages people to think in a nerdy, literal-minded way.

ANSWER:

No. Maybe *you* use it that way but most people who are creative with computers are much more on the **bricolage** side of intellectual style.

WORRY:

Children should run in the sun and the wind instead of being glued to a keyboard.

ANSWER:

Yes. But if you take this argument too literally you won't let them read or play music and certainly won't let them watch movies or television. Or dream.

Balance is everything. But let's be clear about what we are balancing. Running versus sitting is a good issue. Outdoors and indoors as well. But this isn't about computers.

WORRY:

Some computer activities are so attractive that they become addictions and draw the kids away from all other activities that parents can offer them. The worst used to be video games. Now grasshopper-minded surfing and endless chatting in cyberspace meeting places often have the same addictive quality.

ANSWER:

Some people (adults as well as children) do get drawn addictively into mindless activities by computers. Others enjoy the games and the surfing but don't do them to the exclusion of other interests. If people in your family don't want to do anything except games and surfing, you have to look more carefully at the life of your family.

What kind of role model are you? Do you have varied interests yourself? Do you take the children to museums and good theater? Do you read with them? Do you use the computer in varied ways yourself? Are you excited about these activities and about sharing them with the children, or do you do them as a chore? Or perhaps you are *too* excited about them and force them on the children.

Are your children trying to tell you something about being bored or unhappy, or about feeling oppressed?

WORRY:

Using a computer makes kids intellectually lazy by doing the math for them. Anyway they will become dependent on a machine.

EASY ANSWER:

You can get plenty of programs that will drill the number facts into them.

REAL ANSWER:

By using the computer as a **Mathland**, children can do real mathematics instead of the stuff called math at school. Is it worth all that money and psychological damage to program children to simulate a calculator? As for dependence, I'm dependent on these eye glasses and doing pretty well, thank you.

WORRY:

The computer makes children intellectually dependent by encouraging passive-reactive "answering machine" modes of behavior and attitudes to knowledge. The computer programs the kid, and the kid gets used to being programmed.

EASY ANSWER:

That's what School is about (and for most people, work as well) so they might as well get used to it early.

REAL ANSWER:

Let the kids program the computer instead of being programmed by it. Youngsters who are used to taking charge of the computer and of carrying out difficult self-initiated projects will not be in danger of growing up with a sense of helplessness and dependency.

WORRY:

The computer separates the family . . .

ANSWER:

That's up to you.

These worries are just a sample, but they all turn on the same issue: the richness and health of the family. In a healthy family with a strong learning culture, the computer will serve to make what was already good better. In a psychologically unhealthy family with a poor attitude to learning, the computer can aggravate what is already bad. Most families are somewhere in between. The computer is a litmus test that will tell you a lot about where your family stands. Be brave enough to watch it, read the signs and trust your good common sense to know what to do.

# Acknowledgments

It is a Russian custom to consider yourself lucky and make a wish when you can put yourself between two people with the same first name. *The Connected Family* would not exist if I had not been prompted at the beginning and supported through the end by two Suzannes. One is not supposed to tell the wish, but I can't stop them from guessing that it is about them and comes from the bottom of my heart.

Suzanne de Galan has been more than an editor and Suzanne Massie more than a wife in what they gave me and the book. I would not have embarked on such a project if they had not ganged up on me over lobsters on beautiful Deer Isle. And even if I had started, I doubt if I'd have finished it without the patience of the one, the love of the other and the outstanding professional skills of both. And even if I had finished, without their consistently sensible and imaginative advice I would have written something very different—perhaps more stodgy and academic or perhaps more flighty and cute but certainly not what *The Connected Family* became.

I had very few and very slight interactions with others about the work while it was in progress, but these people made a crucial difference: Brian Silverman, always cheerful, smart and supportive; Daniel Dennett, bursting with life and philosophy; Judy McGeorge, who helped me find a sensible fix on the Internet; Carol Sperry, who read an early draft and, as always, gave me sensitive advice about teachers and teaching; Idit Harel, who gave me a shot of inspiration when I most needed it and mobilized the gang at MaMaMedia to help with research and practical details.

Nicholas Negroponte gave me more encouragement than I imagine he knows by agreeing to write a foreword. I was wonderfully surprised by his suggestion that in some ways I had "taught him to think," and all the more so because I so often reflect on how he has taught me to value, and try to emulate, the kind of thinking that he does better than anyone. But perhaps that is the real moral of *The Connected Family*: Learning and teaching are meaningful only when they are mutual.

Many children (Sam says people are children until they are nine) have taught me how to think—and not only about children. The ones who influenced me most as I was writing this book were my grandchildren, John Massie, Samuel Massie and Ian Thomas; my Maine friends, Jessica Bridges, Elise Bishop and Taylor Bishop; and my new email friend, Nicole Sleeth. Nicole represents something special in relation to the themes of this book. A search on the Web for MicroWorlds will find some of Nicole's Logo programming on a page made by her and her father, Dan Sleeth—a model of what I recommend made well ahead of me. I am especially pleased by Nicole's attitude to such things: They are cool enough to do but do not get in the way of her reading or her involvement with friends, sports and nature.

I am very fortunate to have been supported by Janet Bishop in Maine and Florence Williams at M.I.T., who somehow manage to be cheerful as well as professional and efficient in dealing with my changing moods, needs and plans.

# HOT WORD INDEX

# Resource Guide

If I have succeeded at all in my goal of provoking some thought-ful action, readers who have come this far will be looking for resources to support the action and pursue the thinking. This guide will suggest some starting points for what must become, if it is to be of any real use, a self-perpetuating process.

## Our CD-ROM

For those who have a Macintosh or Windows system equipped with a CD-ROM drive, we have provided a CD-ROM with this book that includes demonstration versions of productions by two software publishers. **Logo Computer Systems Inc. (LCSI)** is a company which I helped create as a vehicle for producing soft-ware based closely on my own ideas about children's use of computers. Our CD-ROM contains demonstrations of two LCSI programs, MicroWorlds and *My Make Believe Castle*, both of which I use frequently in the book to illustrate general ideas. **Theatrix Interactive Inc.** provides demonstrations of two pro-ductions: *Juilliard Music Adventure*™ offers children a musical experience related to my own learning described in Chapter 5; *Hollywood*™ is an example of a different constructionist style.

Note: The presentation of MicroWorlds for Windows on the CD-ROM is restricted to an animated demonstration. A version that will allow you to experiment with your own projects can be downloaded from:

http://www.ConnectedFamily.com/Demos

Also available on this site is the iconic version of MicroWorlds mentioned in Chapter 6, plus a great deal of help in using it. To share your projects and ideas go to:

http://www.mamamedia.com/ProjectsTalk

## No CD-ROM Drive?

Some of the content of this CD-ROM, as well as some programs in the same spirit that will run on early model computers, can be obtained on floppy disks or by downloading from Web sites mentioned below. Request information by email to:

info@ConnectedFamily.com

or by writing to:

LONGSTREET PRESS, INC.
2140 Newmarket Parkway
Suite 118
Marietta, GA 30067
re: The Connected Family

## The Web

For those readers who can access the World Wide Web, the best advice I can give is to get better, continuously updated advice (including recommended Web sites) from:

http://www.ConnectedFamily.com

and from another site that I helped create for children (and their parents):

http://www.mamamedia.com

My more academic Web address at the M.I.T. Media Lab is:

http://papert.www.media.mit.edu/people.papert

## Examples of Constructionist Software

Please be aware that the following recommendations are only a sample, and that the suggested ages are *very* approximate indications.

**For preschoolers**
*KidPix*
*My Make Believe Castle*
*Sound Toy*
*Iconic MicroWorlds* (from http://www.ConnectedFamily.com/Demos)

**For seven, plus or minus a few years:**
*SimTower*
*MicroWorlds*
*Widget Workshop*
*The Incredible Toon Machine*
*Making Music*
*Juilliard Music Adventure*™
*Hollywood*™

**For nine, plus or minus a few years:**
*The Incredible Machine*
*MicroWorlds*
*SimCity* (and other Sim-somethings)
*Imagination Express* series
*Storybook Weaver Deluxe*
*Tesselmania*

**Listings of software suitable for children:**
*The Computer Museum: Guide to the Best Software for Kids* (The Boston Computer Museum, tel. 617/426-2800, ext. 322)
*Children's Software Revue: Helping Teachers and Parents Find Software* (tel. 800/993-9499)

## Magazines

There has been a recent mushrooming of magazines devoted to aspects of the digital world. The magazine that best reflects the lifestyle associated with the Internet is *Wired*. Among many magazines that are more focused on computers are *Family PC*, *Home PC*, and *MacHome*.

I am chairman of the advisory board and a contributor to the world's first magazine about the cyberworld for children, *The MaMaMedia Magazine*, which will be launched in early 1997. Before then, you can request a free preview issue by going to:

http://www.mamamedia.com/FreeMagazine

## Books

*Being Digital*, by Nicholas Negroponte
*The End of Education*, by Neil Postman
*Life on the Screen*, by Sherry Turkle
*The Road Ahead*, by Bill Gates
*School's Out*, by Lewis Perelman
*The Second Self*, by Sherry Turkle

**Antecedents of** *The Connected Family:*
*Mindstorms: Children, Computers and Powerful Ideas*, by Seymour Papert
*The Children's Machine: Rethinking School in the Age of the Computer*, by Seymour Papert
*Constructionism*, Idit Harel and Seymour Papert (eds.)

For a more extensive list of books and updates to keep pace with a rapidly changing field, consult:

http://www.ConnectedFamily.com/RelatedReadings

# CD-ROM Instructions

**FOR MORE INFORMATION ABOUT SYSTEM REQUIREMENTS OR RUNNING THIS DEMO, PLEASE CONSULT THE README FILE.**

### Macintosh:
Insert the CD-ROM into your CD-ROM drive.

Double click on the Educational Software Demo icon and follow the instructions on your monitor.

### Windows 3.1/Windows 95
Insert the CD-ROM into your CD-ROM drive.

Select RUN from the Program Manager's File menu (Windows 95 users: Click the start button and select RUN . . .).

In the command Line text box, type: D:/DEMO (if necessary, type the letter address of your CD-ROM drive instead of D:).

Click OK or press ENTER.

This will create a group called Companion CD-ROM in your Program Manager, with an icon called Educational Software Demo. For Windows 95 users, it will create a shortcut in the Start menu and an icon of the same name.

Click the Educational Software Demo icon and follow the instructions on your monitor.